Conflict Resolution

Other titles in the Briefcase Books series include:

To learn more about titles in the Briefcase Books series go to **www.briefcasebooks.com**

You'll find the tables of contents, downloadable sample chapters, information on the authors, discussion guides for using these books in training programs, and more.

A
Briefcase
Book

Conflict Resolution

Mediation Tools for Everyday Worklife

Daniel Dana

McGraw-Hill

New York San Francisco Washington, D.C. Auckland Bogotá
Caracas Lisbon London Madrid Mexico City Milan
Montreal New Delhi San Juan Singapore
Sydney Tokyo Toronto

This is a CWL Publishing Enterprises Book, *developed and produced for
McGraw-Hill by CWL Publishing Enterprises, Inc., Madison, WI,
www.cwlpub.com. Robert Magnan served as editor. For McGraw-Hill, the
sponsoring editor is Catherine Dassopoulos, and the publisher is Jeffrey
Krames.*

Printed and bound by Quad/Graphics, Fairfield

This publication is designed to provide accurate and authoritative information in regard to the subject matter covered. It is sold with the understanding
that neither the author nor the publisher is engaged in rendering legal,
accounting, or other professional service. If legal advice or other expert
assistance is required, the services of a competent professional person
should be sought.

> —*From a Declaration of Principles jointly adopted by a Committee
> of the American Bar Association and a Committee of Publishers*

McGraw-Hill books are available at special quantity discounts to use as pre-
miums and sale promotions, or for use in corporate training programs. For
more information, please write to the Director of Special Sales, McGraw-Hill,
2 Penn Plaza, New York, NY 10121. Or contact your local bookstore.

 This book is printed on recycled, acid-free paper containing a mini-
mum of 50% recycled de-inked fiber.

Contents

Preface

In thinking about and practicing conflict resolution, it's useful to have some historical framework:

- The history of conflict resolution as applied behavioral science began in the 1940s with social psychologist Kurt Lewin and his students at Yale University.
- The history of the behavioral science of conflict resolution as applied to workplaces began in the 1960s with NTL Institute.
- The history of mediation as a non-coercive, interest-based, facilitated process to settle disputes—an alternative to litigation—began in the 1970s. (The legal field prefers to call mediation "ADR"—alternative dispute resolution.)
- The history of mediation as a self-help skill in workplaces began in 1980 with an article outlining managerial mediation in an obscure journal by the present author.
- The history of strategic management of organizational conflict begins with the book you are holding in your hands at this moment.

I recall a conversation with a faculty colleague at the University of Hartford around 1981. Pam was sharing with me her progress in developing a multi-dimensional model of organizational behavior. I was sharing with Pam my emerging view of mediation for non-professionals in the workplace. She remarked, "You know, Dan, the difference between you and me is that I strain for complexity and you strain for simplicity."

Pam did not realize 20 years ago, as she made that astute observation, that she was predicting the course of my career to

the present moment. Nor did I. With planning no more conscious than water coursing its way downhill, I have stumbled
along a career path of simplifying mediation so that everyone—
not just professionals—can enjoy its remarkable benefits.
Milestones along that path are denoted by chapters in this
book—managerial mediation, self-mediation, and preventive
mediation are progressively simpler self-help mediation tools
that everyone can use following only brief study.

Coming of age in the 1960s, I was influenced by the "peace
and love" values of the time—I'm a veteran of both Vietnam and
Woodstock. Over the ensuing decades, I have transformed
those values from Quixotic ideals to practical tools. I declare
this with confidence because the fact that these mediation tools
indeed work is beyond question. My hundreds of corporate
clients and thousands of trainees and students continue to
demonstrate their utility.

This book is the first published treatment of self-help mediation tools for the workplace. It is also the first published exami-
nation of conflict management as a corporate strategic issue.
Later chapters glibly refer to these emergent concepts as a
"paradigm shift"—tongue only lightly planted in cheek. Now
that much of the Earth's population has electronic access to
ideas arising half a world away, it is only a matter of time before
the demonstrable fact that self-help mediation offers a better
way of managing everyday human differences catches on. The
personal, organizational, and societal benefits of doing so are
overwhelming—and they are obvious.

Companies that recognize that internal conflict can be managed strategically will succeed in the global marketplace. Those
that ignore it and incur its unnecessary costs will be at a competitive disadvantage. Companies that failed to recognize quality as a strategic issue 20 years ago either changed or died. I
predict that companies that fail to address conflict as a strategic
issue will meet a similar fate.

A word to my mediator colleagues: those already familiar
with my work over the past two decades know that I've been

pushing the envelope toward mediation-for-everyman (or the gender-inclusive equivalent of that term). My efforts to make mediation accessible to everyone in their everyday lives have been misconstrued by some colleagues as an unwelcome erosion of professionalism in our field. Please read the close of Chapter 1 with particular care. To state my case bluntly: I support the creation and enforcement of standards to protect consumers of professional mediation services. I also support the broadcast sharing of our little secret with the other six billion people on this planet—less to create a consumer market for professional mediators than to empower every individual to apply in their workplaces and their homes what we know how to do. Let's not repeat the misguided error of dentists of decades past who feared that public education about dental hygiene would put dentists out of business. Let's show people how to use self-help mediation, when to call a professional mediator, and how to tell the difference.

I have had fun writing this book, and I hope you have fun reading it. I hope you will actually laugh out loud on occasion—I did while writing. Who says conflict can't be fun!?

I suggest you read it once from start to finish, as later chapters build on blocks laid in earlier ones. Then, return to those chapters that focus on the specific mediation tools that you need to resolve a current conflict.

Special Features

The idea behind the books in the Briefcase Series is to give you practical information written in a friendly person-to-person style. The chapters are short, deal with tactical issues, and include lots of examples. They also feature numerous boxes designed to give you different types of specific information. Here's a description of the boxes you'll find in this book.

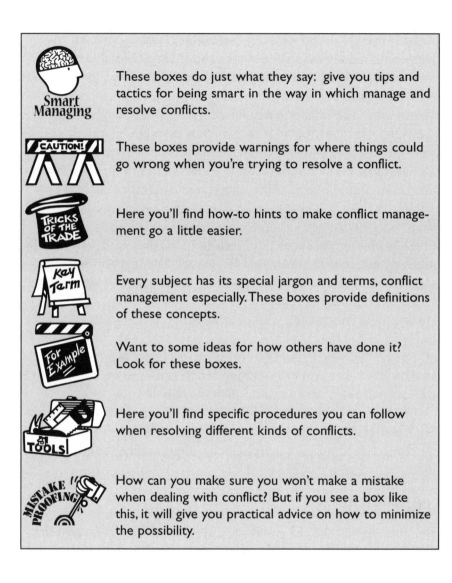

These boxes do just what they say: give you tips and tactics for being smart in the way in which manage and resolve conflicts.

These boxes provide warnings for where things could go wrong when you're trying to resolve a conflict.

Here you'll find how-to hints to make conflict management go a little easier.

Every subject has its special jargon and terms, conflict management especially. These boxes provide definitions of these concepts.

Want to some ideas for how others have done it? Look for these boxes.

Here you'll find specific procedures you can follow when resolving different kinds of conflicts.

How can you make sure you won't make a mistake when dealing with conflict? But if you see a box like this, it will give you practical advice on how to minimize the possibility.

Acknowledgments

Only the most self-absorbed author would claim to have written a book without help. Countless clients, students, teachers, colleagues, and friends have contributed to this work—you know who you are, and you'll recognize your influence in these pages.

I thank my editor, John Woods of CWL Publishing Enterprises, for his confidence and encouragement and for periodically nudging this project back to the top of my to-do list when it was knocked off its proper perch by the onslaught of demands of my day job. I also want to thank Bob Magnan of CWL for his work in editing the manuscript that has actually become this book.

I thank my extended family for lending their names to the characters in this book, and I ask that they infer no hidden meanings from my assignment of their names to their respective namesakes. Most of all, I thank my wife Susan, my daughter Su, and my grandson Seamus for being there in the world, and for being here within me. My audiences sometimes stare in shocked disbelief when I remark that there is no conflict in my life. But we know it's true.

Dan Dana
September, 2000
www.mediationworks.com

About the Author

Dan Dana is a pioneer in the field of mediation. He has pushed the frontier into new territory by reframing mediation as a self-help tool as well as a professional service.

Dan has been a student and practitioner of conflict resolution since the early 1970s. As a graduate student in counseling psychology, he learned a facilitative approach to family systems therapy. Among fellow counseling interns, he became the "go-to guy" for resolving marital conflicts. His doctoral dissertation was on the subject of workplace conflict.

Upon completing the Ph.D. in 1977, Dan developed one of the first Employee Assistance Programs in the federal government under contract with the United States Office of Education (Department of HEW) during the administration of President Jimmy Carter. There, he began to understand that managers and supervisors, with brief training, could perform simple mediation to resolve employee conflicts within their areas of responsibility.

As a professor of organizational behavior at the University of Hartford (Connecticut) in 1978, Dan initiated a graduate MBA course, "Managing Organizational Conflict," which he continues to teach there and at the Summer Institute of Conflict Resolution at Syracuse University (Maxwell School of Government). His course receives the highest student evaluations among all courses in the University of Hartford graduate school of business.

Upon leaving full-time academics in 1985, Dan founded the Mediation Training Institute International, a global network of Certified Trainers who conduct one-day seminars in managerial mediation and self-mediation based on his work. Dan's first book, *Managing Differences,* now published in six languages worldwide, serves as a sourcebook for those seminars.

In 1998, Dana Mediation Institute, Inc., was founded to advance the strategic management of organizational conflict.

He is a popular conference and convention speaker whose most requested keynote title is "Weaving Mediation into the Fabric of Organizations."

Dan resides in Kansas City and works at www.mediation-works.com.

Conflict Resolution

What's a Conflict?

Is This a Conflict?

Seamus is about to graduate from a prestigious university and he already has received two excellent job offers. But he's not happy. What should be a happy situation is tainted by his anxiety about which offer to accept.

The offer from a promising dotcom startup company could be a fabulous opportunity to get in on the ground floor of the next Microsoft. He fantasizes about retiring at age 35 on his own Caribbean Island. But this dotcom could fizzle, like so many other high-tech startups have fizzled, leaving him on the street in a few months looking for a new job.

His other offer is from a *Fortune* 50 smokestack company that has been in business for over a century, so he's sure it won't disappear into thin air as the dotcom might do. But career advancements would be slow. And, he fears being left behind in the technological revolution.

Seamus knows this decision will chart the course of his career for years, if not decades. "What should I do? ... What if I make the wrong decision? ... How can I resolve this conflict?," he cries in anguish.

Is this a conflict?

No. Seamus is torn between two apparently incompatible options about which job to take, but this is not a conflict. His "conflict" is indecision about alternative courses of action, which can be resolved by using good decision-making tools.

Good decision-making helps to prevent conflict. If Seamus takes the wrong job and finds himself unhappy and his unhappiness spills over into his relationships at work, the seeds are sown for conflict.

Is This a Conflict?

Teammates Susan and Sean are struggling with a difficult technical problem. Susan describes to Sean an approach to solving it that she finds compelling. "Doesn't that make sense to you?" she asks, hoping that he is persuaded by her logic.

"You make a good case," agrees Sean, "but I think you've overlooked a critical piece of information. Did you see the memo from the folks over in research that warned about the dangers of doing it that way?"

"Yes, I did," Susan replied. "But they were talking about a very different kind of situation from the one we're dealing with."

They argue back and forth, each teammate adding more information to support his or her position. Each one considers the other's perspective, but they continue to see the problem differently.

Is this a conflict?

Nope. Susan and Sean disagree, but they are not in conflict. Their "conflict" is the absence of agreement about how to solve a problem that they share responsibility for solving. They are communicating well but haven't yet arrived at a shared view of the problem. They need to use good problem-solving tools.

Good problem-solving helps to prevent conflict. If Susan and Sean continue to disagree, they may become frustrated and each may begin to view the other as stubborn, stupid, and incompetent. Once their disagreement is personalized in this way, they've crossed the border into the land of conflict.

Is This a Conflict?

Deana comes home from work totally drained after another hard day at the office. She is nearly in tears with fatigue and frustration. "I don't know if I can take another day in that place," she complains to her husband, Lowell.

"What went on at the office today, honey?" he asks attentively.

"Oh, that noisy construction is still going on across the street, and I found out today that it won't be finished for at least another month," Deana replies. "And the deadline is coming up soon on the big project I've been working on. I'm just not sure I can get it done on time. If I don't, I'll let the whole team down. I'm worried sick that this job just won't work out. I can't take much more of this conflict."

Is this a conflict?

Nope, not this one either. Deana is experiencing a high level of job stress, but her situation is not a conflict. Her "conflict" is her emotional distress about an unpleasant and anxiety-producing situation. She needs to use good stress-management tools.

Good stress management helps to prevent conflict. If Deana's job stress causes her to become irritable and cranky with her coworkers, they may begin to view her as a "difficult person" who is unlikable and unpleasant. Conflict is a short step beyond personal dislike.

Is This a Conflict?

Jon and Donna work closely—or at least they're supposed to. Their desks are close. Jon often gets up from his chair to pace while he's thinking. This drives Donna crazy. "Can't you just sit still for five minutes?," she asks, her voice tight with tension. "Do you have a medical problem? How do you expect me to concentrate with all your commotion?"

"Look, I need to move around to think," Jon retorts angrily. "Besides, what right do you have to complain? You wear that horrendous perfume that pollutes the air I have to breathe. Are

CAUTION!

Conflict? Or Something Else?

Don't confuse conflict with indecision, disagreement, stress, or other common experiences that may cause, or be caused by, conflict. These are not conflict and they are not best handled by conflict-resolution tools.

you trying to cover up the fact that you don't bathe?"

Jon and Donna typically talk this way to each other.

Is this a conflict?

Bingo! Indeed it is. But why? What is it about this last scenario that is different from the first three?

Jon and Donna are experiencing conflict because:

1. *They are interdependent.* That is, each needs something from the other and they are vulnerable if they don't get it. Donna needs a quiet place to work, but Jon's pacing disturbs her. Jon needs to pace in order to think, but Donna's complaints about his movement prevent him from doing so. And . . .

2. *They blame each other.* That is, they find fault with each other for causing the problem. Donna criticizes Jon for being inconsiderate of her need for peace and quiet. Jon criticizes Donna for being unwilling to accept his need to move around. Here, their faultfinding has become personal, going beyond the immediate workplace issue. Donna hints that Jon may have some kind of medical or personal defect that keeps him from working quietly like a "normal" person should. Jon is not so subtle, criticizing Donna's taste in perfume and even questioning her personal hygiene. And . . .

3. *They are angry.* That is, they feel emotionally upset. Donna and Jon are openly angry with each other. But in many conflicts anger is kept hidden. Sometimes we keep up the appearance of politeness and cordiality so well that our coworkers might not even be able to see that we are emotionally upset. Whether hidden or obvious, the emotion we all know as anger is always present when there's a conflict. And . . .

4. *Their behavior is causing a business problem.* That is, each one's productivity and job performance is affected by their lack of cooperation. Both Donna and Jon are distracted from their own work by the other's actions. The fact that they don't like each other, by itself, is not the business problem. The problem that matters to the business is the impact on job performance caused by the behaviors that each one uses as they interact.

> **Workplace conflict** A condition between or among workers whose jobs are interdependent, who feel angry, who perceive the other(s) as being at fault, and who act in ways that cause a business problem.
>
> Notice that this definition includes feelings (emotions), perceptions (thoughts), and actions (behaviors). Psychologists consider these three the only dimensions of human experience. So, conflict is rooted in all parts of our human nature.

If we are going to learn how to resolve conflict, we first need to know what conflict is. Otherwise, we may be using an excellent tool to fix the wrong problem, like the carpenter who tries to drive a nail with a screwdriver. This book describes tools for resolving conflicts that fit this definition.

Kinds of Workplace Conflict

We see in the above scenarios that the word "conflict" is commonly used in everyday speech to label various human experiences, ranging from indecision to disagreement to stress. To be correctly understood as a "conflict," a situation must contain each of the four elements of our definition.

> **If You Don't Know What's Broke ....** Don't assume that as a manager you're responsible for keeping all of your employees happy. Some problems are up to the individual to resolve. Some differences are benign, even beneficial to the work environment. If you haven't thought through the situation, it's smart not to jump into the middle and try to fix it. You may only make it worse.

But there are different types of conflict that fit this definition. They differ in ways that give us clues about how they can be resolved. We need to understand what kind of conflict we're dealing with before we can select the appropriate conflict-resolution tool to resolve it.

Let's use the word "structure" to refer to the ways that we can analyze conflicts. We must first understand the *structure* of a conflict to decide how to resolve it successfully. Fortunately, there are only six parts of conflict structure that we need to pay attention to:

1. **Interdependency.** How much do the parties need each other to act cooperatively, to provide resources, or to provide satisfaction of other needs? If interdependency is high, then the costs of not resolving it are also likely to be high. (See Chapter 2 for a way to measure the financial cost of unresolved conflict.) If interdependency is low, then "watchful waiting" may be an appropriate conflict-management strategy. If there were absolutely *no* interdependency, then conflict wouldn't exist at all. So, by definition, conflict occurs only between parties who need each other and who cannot simply leave the relationship with no negative consequences.

2. **Number of interested parties.** How many distinct parties—individuals or groups—have an interest in how the conflict is resolved? If there are only two parties in conflict, and those parties are individuals, resolving it can often be surprisingly easy and quick. As the number and size of parties increase, there are more people to please and the difficulty of resolving the conflict increases.

3. **Constituent representation.** Do the parties represent the interests of other people ("constituents") who are not personally and directly involved in the process of resolving the conflict? When we speak only for ourselves and do not have to please others who are not present and involved, resolution is much easier. Reaching an agreement that is acceptable to everyone who is affected by how the issue is

resolved, especially those who are not personally involved, is more difficult.

4. **Negotiator authority.** If the parties consist of more than one individual, say a department within an organization, is the person or team of people who represent the interests of that department able to make concessions or reach creative solutions without going back to their constituents for approval? If negotiator authority is high, then resolution is easier. If negotiator authority is low, then the process of resolving the conflict will take longer and will be more difficult.

5. **Critical urgency.** Is it absolutely necessary that a solution be found in the very near future, i.e., in the next few minutes or hours, to prevent a disaster? Or is there time to talk together for an extended time to find the best solution? Even better, is there no immediate crisis at all, allowing people to interact with each other in ways that *prevent* conflicts from arising in the first place? The greater the critical urgency, the less likely a consensual solution.

6. **Communication channels.** Are the parties able to talk to each other face to face in the same room? If this is not possible, can they talk voice to voice on the telephone? Or must they talk keyboard to keyboard by using real-time (synchronous) Internet technology, such as an on-line conference or chat room? Or is it necessary that they communicate back and forth using an asynchronous technology, such as e-mail? Same-time-same-place dialogue nearly always produces far better solutions than lesser communication channels.

Every manager, from time to time, has to deal

Conflict structure The dimensions or elements that allow analysis of conflict, resulting in ability to decide how best to resolve it. Conflict structure consists of:
- Interdependency
- Number of interested parties
- Constituent representation
- Negotiator authority
- Critical urgency
- Communication channels

with conflicts that are defined by a variety of structures. Let's take several kinds of workplace conflicts and examine their structure.

Interpersonal Conflict

The conflict between Donna and Jon is an "interpersonal conflict," which is the simplest and easiest kind to resolve. And it is the most common kind of conflict in workplaces.

Two mediation tools—managerial mediation and self-mediation—are designed to resolve interpersonal conflicts and will be described in future chapters. Using these tools results in a mutually acceptable solution to the business problem about nine out of 10 times. Considering that the success rate of conflict avoidance is zero, that's pretty impressive!

Returning to our tale of woe, I'll introduce you to Edna, who is Donna and Jon's manager. Edna, whose office is just down the hall from their workstations, is very aware of the conflict between her two employees. She's overheard their arguments firsthand. Their coworkers have also come to her to complain about the tension between Donna and Jon and about how much it interferes with their own work. Edna recognizes that Donna and Jon are both good workers who try to do their best, but the tension between them is causing their job performance and productivity to suffer.

Edna can use managerial mediation to resolve their dispute so Donna and Jon can get back to working together effectively. Chapter 4 will explain exactly how Edna is going to accomplish this feat.

But first, Edna will think about the structure of conflict between Donna and Jon. She'll ask herself these six questions:

Are they interdependent? Yes, each one needs the other to avoid doing things that disturb his or her concentration. If Donna or Jon could be simply relocated so they were not near each other and their work redesigned so their job tasks were unrelated (that is, eliminate their interdependency), the conflict would disappear. Otherwise, they remain highly interdependent.

Managerial mediation A dialogue tool for use by managers, supervisors, team leaders, and others that involves a simple form of third-party mediation to resolve conflict between two employees for whose performance the manager is responsible.

How many interested parties? Only two—Jon and Donna. Their coworkers want their conflict to be resolved, so they won't be distracted by their public clashes, but the coworkers don't have a stake (an interest) in *how* it is resolved.

Do they represent constituencies? No. Their coworkers want the problem to be solved, but Donna and Jon don't have to get approval from coworkers for how they decide to do that.

Do they have authority to negotiate on behalf of their own interests? Absolutely. Since there are no constituencies, there's no one to please but themselves.

Is this an urgent crisis? Nope. Their behavior is affecting performance and productivity, but no disaster looms on the horizon. Although their conflict is happening in the moment, it's not a crisis—if they don't resolve it today, they'll just spat again tomorrow.

Can they communicate face to face? Certainly. They are in the same physical area, so direct (same-time-same-place) communication is possible.

No Third Party?

But what if Edna doesn't know about the conflict between Donna and Jon? Maybe her office is in another building, or another city, far away. Or maybe she just doesn't know how to deal with it, and so buries her head in the sand. Does the conflict stay unresolved?

Not necessarily. Either Donna or Jon can use a mediation tool, self-mediation, that doesn't involve a third party. If either employee knew about the tool and chose to use it, he or she could initiate a dialogue with the other.

> **Key Term** **Self-mediation** A dialogue tool for use by individuals who are personally involved in conflict with another person with whom they have an ongoing, interdependent relationship. The self-mediator performs the essential functions of a third-party mediator while also representing his or her own interests that are at stake in the dispute.

The initiator of self-mediation plays two roles: first, as a negotiator who is trying to get his or her own interests satisfied, and second, as a mediator who is doing some simple tasks that a third-party mediator would do, if a third party were present. But remember: Edna has her head in the sand and no one else is there to mediate. So, Donna or Jon can mediate.

Imagine that you are either Jon or Donna and that your manager, Edna, is on the other side of the planet. It's up to you to mediate this conflict with your frustrating coworker. If you choose to use self-mediation, you would be the one who analyzes the conflict structure. Would you arrive at the same answers as Edna? Yes, you would. Structure is a property of the conflict, not of the mediator. Structure is in the nature of the conflict itself.

Team Conflict

Let's look at a conflict with a slightly different structure.

Karen leads a six-member project team that was created to develop a new insurance product and bring it to market. Each member brings a special expertise to the project, but their tasks must be carefully coordinated so that time is not wasted by any member going one direction while the rest of the team is going another. So, the team meets at least once a day for each member to give progress reports to the others.

A conflict has developed between the members of the team who are conducting market research and those who are designing the pricing structure of the new product. Over the past several days, the team's meetings have become increasingly divisive. Todd, who heads the pricing sub-team, complains that

Jeanine, who heads the market research sub-team, is not collecting market data quickly enough.

"My people have a deadline for submitting the pricing structure to top management," Todd declares, "and we aren't going to have time to run the necessary tests unless you get the market data to us. That's going to make us look really bad. Hurry it up, will you!"

Jeanine retorts, "We can't help it if the market sample we have to study are busy people with jobs to do. They aren't just sitting by their phones waiting for us to call. We sometimes have to play telephone tag for days before we're able to reach them. So don't blame us for things we don't have any control over!"

Todd and Jeanine lead the argument and the rest of the team falls in behind them. Karen realizes that a serious rift is developing on her team that endangers its success.

Let's help Karen think about the structure of the conflict she faces. In most respects the structure is similar to the interpersonal conflict between Donna and Jon. But there is one main difference—the number of interested parties. That difference has a big impact on which mediation tool Karen should select to resolve the conflict.

Now, let's change another part of the structure of the conflict in Karen's team. What if team members were themselves heads of departments or work units? So, each team member is responsible and accountable to a number of other people (a constituency). Would this change how Karen approached the conflict on her team?

> **Team mediation** A dialogue tool for use by team leaders for resolving disputes among members that involves the leader acting as a low-power, neutral third party.
>
> **Smart Managing**

Indeed it would! As representatives of constituencies, team members may have varying degrees of negotiator authority, the power that a constituency gives its representative to make compromises and engage in a give-and-take exchange to solve the team problem. Karen's task as mediator would be a lot more complicated and challenging if team members had little negotiator authority.

Conflict Prevention

Let's turn back the clock on Karen's team conflict several weeks or months. What might she have done to prevent the crisis that now threatens the survival of her team?

Might she have established certain skills, behavioral norms, and shared expectations that would have enabled members of her team to deal constructively with their differences?

In two words, "very likely." Karen may have been able to practice "preventive mediation" so that the destructive and costly conflict she faces today would never have happened. We'll look more closely at preventive mediation in Chapter 7.

Analyzing Conflicts

So, we now understand that the structure of conflict can vary widely. The mediation tools that are explained in this book will enable you resolve some, but not all, conflicts. Clearly, resolving an international dispute or settling a baseball players' strike is beyond our scope. Let's get a better idea of what kinds of conflicts you'll be prepared to resolve and what kinds you'd better refer to a professional mediator.

A Conflict Analysis Worksheet

Use this worksheet to help you analyze the structure of a conflict that you are dealing with now.

Preventive mediation A dialogue tool for use by members and leaders of working groups that applies two guiding principles drawn from the practice of mediation and enables non-adversarial management of differences in all important relationships.

Circle the number that most accurately reflects the conflict situation. Scoring instructions are below.

Interdependency
1 = low (the parties need to interact occasionally to get their jobs done)
2 = medium (the parties interact frequently to exchange information or resources)
3 = high (the parties interact daily and have a high need for voluntary cooperation to do their jobs satisfactorily)

Number of interested parties
1 = two parties
3 = three or four parties
5 = five or more parties

Constituent representation
1 = none (each party is an individual who is not negotiating on behalf of others)
2 = one or two other people are being represented by the individuals who are involved in resolving the conflict
3 = several other people constitute an identifiable team or group that is being represented by individuals who are directly involved in negotiations
7 = a large disorganized group is being represented

Negotiator authority
1 = absolute (parties are individuals without constituents or they do not need to get prior approval from constituents to make compromises with other parties)
3 = high (parties may make compromises with confidence that constituents will agree)

5 = low (parties may offer compromises but need to check with constituents for approval)

7 = none (parties can only deliver messages from constituents)

Critical urgency

1 = none (the current situation, although not desirable, can continue
indefinitely without causing great harm)

2 = urgent (a solution must be reached in the next few days)

6 = crisis (a solution must be reached immediately, in the next few
minutes or hours)

Communication channels

1 = parties can meet face to face (same time, same place)

3 = parties can meet only by telephone or videoconference (same
time, different place)

5 = parties can only write asynchronous messages (different time, different place)

Scoring

Add the numbers that you have circled while having in mind a particular conflict that you want to resolve. The possible range is from 6 to
33. The lower the number, the more likely it is that you can resolve
the conflict yourself by using the mediation tools provided in this
book. The higher the number, the more likely it is that you may need a
professional mediator to resolve it satisfactorily.

What Is Mediation?

Readers who are already knowledgeable about mediation may
be puzzled—even shocked—that I'm using the term to refer to
ways of resolving conflicts without the involvement of a third
party. Mediation is usually defined as a process that necessarily
involves the participation of a neutral third party (a "mediator")
who helps disputing parties find solutions to contested issues.

Let me explain your puzzlement and ease your shock.

Mediation is an emerging field of professional practice. Most
mediators come from other professional fields—such as psychology, social work, counseling, employee relations, and law—
that license their members. That is, individuals must demonstrate a defined level of competency to be permitted to offer

Self mediation or than 3rd party

paid professional services to consumers. Mediation is on its way to becoming such a field.

But most professions that license their practitioners recognize that there exists a core body of knowledge and skill that the general public may learn and use for their own benefit, without paying for the services of a professional. For example, self-health care is widely accepted. All of us "practice medicine" by getting rest and drinking lots of fluids when we feel a cold coming on. We also "practice psychology" when we listen compassionately to a friend who is feeling sad, lonely, or anxious due to a difficult life situation. Unless a medical or psychological problem reaches a certain level of severity, we don't need to pay a physician or psychotherapist for these services. We can do it ourselves, once we know the basics—and the limits—of that field of professional service.

The same is true of mediation. Daily newspaper headlines report conflicts in business, in society, and around the world that challenge the abilities of the most expert mediators. But in our daily work lives, we can "practice mediation" once we know the basics—and the limits—of the field.

This book gives you, the manager, a basic knowledge of mediation that enables you to use some of the tools of the professional practitioner to manage conflicts in your area of responsibility. It also alerts you to the limits of "self-help mediation" so you can call a professional when you recognize that the mediation tools in this book are likely not to be effective.

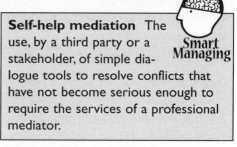

Self-help mediation The use, by a third party or a stakeholder, of simple dialogue tools to resolve conflicts that have not become serious enough to require the services of a professional mediator.

Smart Managing

So, managerial mediation, self-mediation, team mediation, and preventive mediation are the names given to self-help mediation tools that managers can use in their jobs. Reading this book and using these dialogue tools does not make you a professional mediator, any more than reading a medical self-help book makes you a physician. It's been estimated that 90% of health problems can be prevented or managed by wise choices that we can make about our own health—eating a balanced diet, exercising regularly, maintaining positive social and family relationships, avoiding tobacco, drugs, and excessive alcohol, etc. By making wise choices about how we handle conflicts, especially before they escalate and become crises, we can also prevent or manage an equal percentage of conflicts. In this book I intend to give you the information you need to make wise choices.

Manager's Checklist for Chapter 1

❏ The word "conflict" is commonly used in everyday speech to label situations that are not really conflicts. We need to know what conflict is before we can successfully resolve it. It must involve a condition between or among workers whose jobs are interdependent, who feel angry, who perceive the other(s) as being at fault, and who act in ways that cause a business problem.

❏ Different kinds of conflicts have different structural properties, depending on six dimensions or elements: interdependency, number of interested parties, constituent representation, negotiator authority, critical urgency, and communication channels. The mediation tools explained in this book are designed to help you resolve conflicts with some kinds of structure, but not others.

❏ Mediation can be done by people who are not mediators. Indeed, every manager can use the self-help mediation tools described in this book to resolve conflicts for which they are designed without additional training.

So What if There's Conflict?

Being in conflict is no fun. It's stressful, unpleasant, distract-ing, intrusive, and annoying.

But is that all?

Roy, Karen's manager, is sitting at his desk pondering the problem on Karen's team. Roy is a strictly-business, no-non-sense, get-the-widgets-out-the-door kind of manager. He's thinking, "OK, so what if conflict is no fun? We aren't here to have fun. We're here to get the job done. I can't be bothered with conflict between my employees if all it does is make peo-ple a little uncomfortable. I'm not running a resort here. Get over it!"

Let's see if we can get Roy's attention about how conflict is affecting his organization.

Costs: Money Down the Drain

Conflict costs money. Does that get your attention, Roy? He pulls a copy of his company's budget out of a folder and scans down the column of expense items. Is "conflict" on the list? Almost certainly not. But other budget line items—some pretty big ones—are there, and conflict is nested within them.

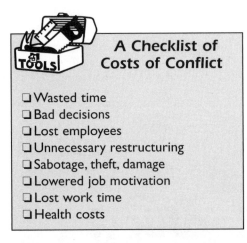

A Checklist of Costs of Conflict

❑ Wasted time
❑ Bad decisions
❑ Lost employees
❑ Unnecessary restructuring
❑ Sabotage, theft, damage
❑ Lowered job motivation
❑ Lost work time
❑ Health costs

How about "staff salaries," for example? Let's dig beneath the surface of that document in Roy's hands to see how conflict costs money, even though it's not listed as an expense item.

Later in this chapter you'll find a worksheet for estimating the financial cost of workplace conflict. In the next few pages, we'll look at the eight cost factors that appear on that worksheet. As we calculate the cost of conflict on Karen's team, you might like to use the worksheet to estimate the cost of an actual conflict that's going on right now in your own organization. But be sure you're sitting down—you could be in for a shock.

Wasted Time

Time is money. Organizations pay employees for their time. So when time is wasted, money is wasted.

How much time is wasted by interpersonal conflict? Let's do some calculations using the situation in Karen's team of six people. Let's say they spend half of their hour-long daily meetings arguing unproductively, which is time that would be used constructively if they were working cooperatively. That amounts to three wasted person-hours each day.

What's that time costing the company? Let's say their annual salaries average $50,000 and an eight-hour workday is expected. Considering weekends, holidays, vacations, and other excused absences, they actually work 200 days each year. That means that their average hourly cost to the company is $31.25 in salary alone. But health insurance, retirement plans, and other fringe benefits add about 50% to salary cost. So, the actual average hourly cost of the team members is $46.87. Consequently, the cost of this conflict is $140.61 for each day it remains unresolved. That's $703.05 each week, or $2812.20 each month, or $9139.65 a quarter, or …. Well, you get the idea. And that's only the cost of the time spent arguing during their meetings.

But this team conflict is wasting valuable time in other ways. What about the amount of time the members of Karen's team spend stewing about the conflict while they are trying to work back at their desks? And what about the time talking with team-mates with whom they agree about the teammates with whom they don't agree?

Research studies show that up to 42% of employees' time is spent engaging in or attempting to resolve conflict. Let's con-servatively estimate that Karen's team members spend only 25% of their time this way.

Using the same assump-tions as above, this means that another $562.44 is wasted every day the con-flict continues unresolved. Adding this to the unpro-ductive time arguing dur-ing meetings, the cost of wasted time in this conflict is $703.05 every day, $3515.25 every week, $14,061 every month, or $168,732 for a fiscal year.

> **Be Conservative**
>
> Use conservative esti-mates in calculating the cost of conflict, especially if you are preparing a report for senior execu-tives to justify the expense of training or a strategic conflict management program in your company. Don't give them an easy way to discount your argument—a conservative estimate will be impressive enough!

Got your attention yet, Roy?

Bad Decisions

Every employee at every level makes decisions on the job. Some decisions are simple and nearly automatic and don't have much impact. Other decisions, especially those made by key employees and managers, can have significant financial conse-quences. In fact, employees' salaries generally correlate with the bottom-line importance of decisions they're responsible for making.

Making *any* decision, requires that you have relevant information. An uninformed decision is usually a bad one.

Recall the fable about the man in ancient times who was forced to choose to open one of two doors. Behind one door was a beautiful princess; behind the other was a hungry tiger. How could the man decide? Of course, with no information to guide his selection, it could only be arbitrary. And the consequences (costs) of making the wrong decision would be disastrous.

How do employees get the information they need to make the best decision? Usually, their coworkers and other employees who perform related functions are key information sources.

Now, what happens when there is unresolved conflict between a decision-maker and an information source? Can the decision-maker trust the coworker to provide objective, valid, sufficient, and accurate information? Or might the coworker's feelings of anger and resentment cause him or her to distort that information or to hold back? There's a high risk that the angry coworker, who regards their relationship as adversarial, will withhold and/or manipulate the information that the decision-maker needs. Should the man who must choose between the lady and the tiger trust the advice of the princess's other suitor?

But conflict contaminates the decision-making process in even more serious ways than causing information to be incomplete or unreliable. Most important decisions are made jointly by several people. Rarely does only one individual, even a top executive, have sole responsibility for making a decision. This is especially true in today's team-based organizations.

Now, what if there is unresolved conflict between decision-makers? Are they going to be purely and unequivocally motivated by what is best for their organization? Almost certainly not. Each decision-maker's judgment and objectivity will surely be affected if he or she feels threatened by the apparent intentions of the others. It is very likely that individuals' needs to protect their self-esteem, to preserve their power, to maintain their social

status within the work group, and to be proven right by the outcome will override their objectivity, regardless of how loyal and
well-intentioned they may be. We are human, and human nature
compels us to protect ourselves in risky circumstances.
Although our physical safety is rarely at risk in workplace conflicts, our underlying interests and needs are always in jeopardy.

As a result, decisions made jointly by two or more people
who are embroiled in unresolved conflict will be imperfect at
best—and seriously flawed at worst.

Let's consider the impact of the conflict on Karen's team on
decision quality. They must make several decisions. They must
decide how to develop a pricing strategy in the absence of complete market data. They must decide how to maximize the value
of the incomplete market data in hand until complete data are
available. They must decide how to respond to top management's imperative that everyone sign off on the progress report
that's due at noon today. None of these decisions can be made
by only one person, not even Karen. The team members are
interdependent decision-makers.

Clearly, how the team decides these issues will impact the
quality of the project team's output as well as the bottom line of
the company. The team may even become paralyzed by the
conflict and fail to decide at all. It's impossible to calculate the
exact dollar amount of that impact. The impact of conflict on
quality of decision-making is not as easy to quantify as the
amount of time wasted due to conflict.

A reasonable approach to this calculation is to estimate the
net sales revenue during a fiscal year from the new product if
the team performs as hoped and then to compare that with a
sales estimate if the team's performance is impaired by poor
decision-making due to the unresolved conflict. Let's assign figures of $100,000 and $50,000, respectively, to those two estimates. These estimates are probably very much lower than the
actual figures of a company with annual sales of several million
dollars. But, being conservative, let's say the cost of poor decision-making due to the conflict on Karen's team is $50,000.

The annual cost of unresolved conflict on Karen's team, summing the first two cost factors, is $218,732.

Got your attention yet, Roy?

Lost Employees

Organizations invest in employees' skills by paying a premium salary and by training them. Exit interviews, which explore departing employees' underlying reasons for quitting, reveal that chronic unresolved conflict is a decisive factor in at least 50% of all voluntary departures. And conflict accounts for up to 90% of the cause of involuntary terminations, with the exception of staff reductions due to downsizing, mergers, and restructuring.

Raytheon Corporation determined that replacing an engineer costs the company 150% of the departing employee's total annual compensation—the combination of salary and benefits. Analysts arrived at this figure by accounting for lost productivity, recruiting fees, interviewing time, staffing department employees' salaries, and orientation and training costs. So, replacing an employee whose annual salary is $50,000 and whose fringe benefits amount to another $25,000 costs the employer $112,500.

Kevin is a member of Karen's team. He was recently approached by a headhunter who offered him a similar position at another company for slightly higher pay. Kevin wouldn't leave a job simply for a small pay increase. He likes his current job and enjoys most of the people he works with, but the ongoing tension on this team is wearing him down. Believing that life is too short to put up with the hassle, and seeing no improvement on the horizon, Kevin accepts the headhunter's offer.

Kevin's choice to leave is not entirely attributable to the conflict on the team. Let's give it about 50% weight in his balancing of the two options—staying or leaving. So, Kevin's decision to go to greener and more peaceful pastures costs the company $56,250 in replacement costs.

Our running total of the first three cost factors is now $274,982.

Got your attention yet, Roy?

Unnecessary Restructuring

Managers sometimes restructure the design and flow of tasks to reduce interaction between conflicting employees. Usually, the original task design was created because that was the logical way to get the work done, assuming that employees could work together cooperatively. So, work that is restructured to avoid a "people problem" is usually less efficient.

Karen, hoping to reduce tension between Todd and Jeanine, instructs all members of the team to channel their emails and other communications through her. She hopes that monitoring and filtering out inflammatory messages that are being tossed back and forth between the two camps like grenades will stanch the bleeding of the team's productivity.

While this modified work design may reduce conflict by reducing interaction, it also removes opportunities for collaboration and creative problem-solving that would have occurred if the two sub-teams had been able to work cooperatively. It also places a greater burden on Karen's time to act as the intermediary for all their communications. And messages get stuck in a bottleneck and are delayed in reaching the recipient because Karen can't always be available to immediately review and forward them.

So how much does this restructuring cost the company? Again, we can't precisely quantify the resulting inefficiency. A conservative assumption is that the cost is about 10% of the combined salaries of employees whose relationship was restructured, for the time the restructuring is in effect.

Recall that Karen's team members receive an average annual compensation of $75,000 each (salary plus benefits). Ten percent of the combined labor cost to the company of the seven individuals (Karen and her six employees) is $52,500.

Our running total for the first four cost factors is now $327,482.

Got your attention yet, Roy?

Sabotage, Theft, and Damage

Studies reveal a direct correlation between prevalence of employee conflict and the amount of damage and theft of inventory and equipment. And covert sabotage of work processes often occurs when employees feel angry toward their employer. Much of the cost incurred by this factor is hidden from management's view, often excused as "accidental" or "inadvertent" errors. This cost is almost certainly greater than you realize.

Let's peer inside the minds of Karen's team members. Todd and Jeanine are getting more and more resentful of the other's stubborn refusal to understand that his or her demands are unrealistic. Each one is becoming more entrenched in a win-lose view of the problem and fair compromise is a fading hope. They are becoming desperate as they see their careers and reputations being jeopardized.

Let's remember that Todd and Jeanine are both competent, professional, ethical employees who want to do a good job. They are not evil saboteurs. But they are human—and they feel increasingly backed into a corner. Traits acquired through eons of human history compel us to fight back when we feel cornered with no way out.

How do Todd and Jeanine fight back? Todd decides to take matters into his own hands and hack into Jeanine's computer for access to the market pool database that her sub-team is trying to reach by telephone. He's particularly interested in the people who have not yet returned her calls. Being active in community theater, he secretly asks a couple of actor friends, who are able to disguise their voices, to "return" calls to Jeanine's people, giving them "data" for her market research. As long as his pricing design is based on the numbers that she provides, he can't be blamed for anything that goes wrong later. Besides, he thinks he knows pretty well how the market pool will respond anyway, so he believes he's not harming the finished product.

Meanwhile, Jeanine, who is no computer slouch herself, hacks into Todd's computer and erases the work that his sub-team has accomplished so far on the pricing design. She figures

---

A Time Bomb

A former computer network administrator was found guilty in May 2000 of intentionally causing irreparable damage to his company's computer system. He created a "time bomb" program that permanently deleted all of the high-tech manufacturer's sophisticated manufacturing programs. The damage, lost contracts, and lost productivity totaled more than $10 million.

Why did he do it? He got demoted after working for the company for about 10 years. He soon began developing the bomb—which he set off two weeks after he got terminated the following year.

---

that by the time they reconstruct their work, she'll be able to gather the market data needed to complete the project. Consequently, she can't be blamed for holding up the team and being responsible for any failure.

Todd and Jeanine may feel a bit guilty about their deceptive tactics, but they believe their actions are justified by the obstructive and uncooperative behavior of the other. In their minds, Todd and Jeanine think their stealthy tactics are ultimately beneficial to the organization. (Does this remind you of patriotic politicians who explain that their votes for pork barrel spending are forced by the partisan intransigence of the opposing political party?)

How do we calculate the financial cost of this sabotage? Again, not precisely. But it clearly has a bottom-line impact on the company. An approach to measuring it is to assign a percentage of the net annual sales of the product that is affected. Let's be conservative and assume that Todd's and Jeanine's sabotage cost 10% of the expected $100,000 annual sales of the new insurance product, for a total of $10,000.

Our running total of the first five cost factors is now $337,482.

Got your attention yet, Roy?

Lowered Job Motivation

From time to time, most employees' motivation to do a good job is eroded by the unrelieved stress of trying to get along with a "difficult person." Todd and Jeanine are likely not the only members of Karen's team who see certain teammates as "difficult people" whose mental health seems uncertain. (After all, how could a sane person act so crazy?) From our comfortable perch as objective observers high above the battlefield, we readers can recognize that Todd and Jeanine are capable employees who are motivated to do a good job. We can appreciate that conflict makes good people look like difficult people.

Once again, this is an effect of workplace conflict that is difficult to quantify and impossible to measure precisely, yet inarguably has a financial impact.

Recall our calculation of the total annual cost of employment of the seven team members, including Karen, as $525,000—that is, seven times $75,000. Let's estimate that each team member's lowered job motivation, averaged over the course of a year, cut his or her productivity by 5%. Surely, for some periods during that year they were all enthusiastic contributors to the team's goals who were working at top efficiency. But at other times, their motivation may have been deeply eroded. Five percent is an estimate of the average over the year. So, lowered job motivation in Karen's team costs $26,250.

Our running total for the first six cost factors is now $363,732.

Got your attention yet, Roy?

Lost Work Time

Absenteeism is associated with job stress, particularly the stress of chronic conflict with coworkers. This stress—mixed in a witch's brew with ingredients such as disregard for how one's absence impacts coworkers, stressors arising from one's personal life, and other foul-smelling factors—leads to employees' choosing to take time off.

Be honest: have you ever taken a "sick day" when you weren't really sick? You may have simply needed a "mental health break" from the daily grind of dealing with a micromanaging supervisor or an intolerably annoying coworker.

But maybe you really were sick when you took that sick day. Medical science has uncovered some very interesting facts about illness. We now know that nearly every physical illness and injury, from viral infections to cancer to workplace accidents, is partially "psychogenic." That is, they are caused in part by psychological or emotional conditions.

This doesn't mean that an illness is "all in your head." It means that your immune system was weakened by stress, permitting the virus to enter your body. It means that being preoccupied with a conflict caused you to be more susceptible to distractions while operating heavy equipment, making you more likely to be injured.

Clearly, the stress of conflict is not the single cause of your illness or injury: the virus really was hammering at the door of your immune system; the heavy equipment really was dangerous to operate. But conflict is one contributor that combines with other factors to cause illnesses and injuries, resulting in lost work time.

Once more, the exact amount of that contribution is impossible to calculate. And, once again, it undoubtedly causes financial cost. Let's estimate, again conservatively, that this cost is about 5% of the combined annual salaries of the affected employees.

Karen has noticed that members of her team have been taking more days off lately. So, we'll figure that the cost of lost work time for Karen's team is 5% of $525,000, or $26,250 annually.

Our running total for the first seven cost factors is now $389,982.

Got your attention yet, Roy?

Health Costs

Aside from lost work time resulting from illness and injury, the medical care provided to ill and injured employees costs the company money in another way. Since the rate of claims affects the premium paid by an employer to its health insurance provider, those payments are an indirect cost of workplace conflict.

What is the likely contribution that conflict-related job stress makes to causing illnesses and injuries that require medical attention under the employer's insurance plan? Again, an exact

calculation is impossible. Depending on the plan's deductibles
and whether employees have families, the yearly cost per
employee ranges between $3000 and $10,000. So, the annual
cost for Karen's team is between $21,000 and $70,000. Her
employees are young, healthy, single people who pay a high
deductible. We can conservatively say that the annual increase
of cost of medical care that's attributable to workplace conflict
is 5% of the low end of that scale. So, the visits that members of
Karen's team make to doctors—not only psychiatrists and psychological counselors who treat explicitly diagnosed psychological disorders—cost her company $1,050 annually.

The total for these eight cost factors is now $391,032.

Got your attention yet, Roy?

Calculating the Cost in Your Organization

Karen's organization is a mid-size firm that employs white collar
workers in a service industry. Your company may be larger or
smaller. Yours may be a manufacturing company, a high-tech
firm, a government agency, a nonprofit social services organization, a family business, or a hospital. Use the guidelines above
to calculate the cost of one particular conflict that you are
closely familiar with. Estimate conservatively ... but still be prepared for a shock!

Legal Costs

You may be thinking, "But wait a minute! Where do the lawyers
come in? I hear a lot about high legal costs, but that isn't
included as a cost factor in this analysis."

This book deals with conflicts that happen in the everyday
lives of managers at work. Those that rise to a level that
involves attorneys impose even greater costs. Let's distinguish
between *formal* and *informal* conflicts.

Formal disputes are those in which employees have filed a
grievance or hired a lawyer to represent them. Formal disputes
incur costs beyond those listed on our worksheet—and not just
attorney fees. Salaries of employee/labor relations staff to admin-

Cost Estimation Worksheet	
Cost Factors	**Estimated Cost**
1. Wasted time	$_____
2. Reduced decision quality	$_____
3. Loss of skilled employees	$_____
4. Restructuring	$_____
5. Sabotage/theft/damage	$_____
6. Lowered job motivation	$_____
7. Lost work time	$_____
8. Health costs	$_____
Total Cost:	$_____

ister grievances, executives whose time is diverted to arbitrate complaints, and fees paid to external arbitrators are only three of the extra costs generated by formal conflicts.

Informal conflicts are those everyday problems that most managers simply take for granted as an unwelcome fact of life with employees. (A frustrated supervisor once remarked, "I'd really like being in management if it weren't for all these pesky employees!")

Formal conflicts Conflicts that have officially involved mediators, arbitrators, attorneys, employee relations staff, or other dispute resolution professionals.
Informal conflicts Conflicts that have involved no such outside parties in the conflict resolution process.

Although formal disputes receive the most public attention, they represent only the tip of the iceberg of the cost of conflict. Despite our pulling of hair and gnashing of teeth about legal costs, attorney fees, and other expenses in settling formal disputes probably represent less than 10% of the total cost of conflict to an organization.

Here's a true story. Tara, a mid-level executive of a large telecommunications company, attended a seminar presented in her company by Dan, a mediator-consultant in the area. Tara and Dan bumped into each other at a neighborhood health club shortly following the seminar. After exchanging pleasantries, Tara mentioned that a lawsuit had recently been filed against her company by a major vendor, alleging breach of contract and asking for $5 million in damages. Dan asked whether the company was considering mediation as an alternative to litigation. Tara found the idea interesting and said she would propose the idea to senior executives.

A few weeks later Tara and Dan again ran into each other at the health club. Tara reported that the company had decided to "let the legal department handle it."

Several months later, when Tara and Dan again ran into each other at the club, Tara reported happily that "we won the suit." Dan asked whether the company had a way of accounting for the internal costs of the litigation. Tara promised to find out.

The next time the two met, Tara reported that "winning" the lawsuit cost her company over $1 million. A mediator's fee for settling the dispute probably would have been under $5,000. (Of course, this doesn't count any settlement amount determined through mediation.)

How Much Can Be Saved?

Even the most effective conflict management practices cannot completely eliminate the financial cost. Just as it takes money to make money, it takes time to save time. Just as we incur costs— medical checkups, exercise facility fees, books about health care and the time to read them, and better-quality food, to name a few—to reduce the far greater cost of serious illness, organizations incur costs in preventing and resolving workplace conflict. Training, education, and planning require time and money.

It's an investment. Expensive formal disputes escalate from informal conflicts that could have been more easily and inexpensively resolved. Every tree was once a sapling, every adult was once a child, and every formal dispute was once an informal conflict.

So how much can an organization realistically expect to save by strategically managing its informal conflicts? Again, no hard numbers are available to answer that question. But a thoughtful analysis of the financial cost of conflict by using the tools in this chapter yields a conservative estimate that 10% to 50% of the total cost could be saved.

So, Karen's company could have saved $40,000 to $200,000 by effectively resolving just the one conflict that we examined on her team. How many similar conflicts are going on in the company?

Got your attention yet, Roy?

Risks: Torpedo Submarines in Our Midst

Sometimes really, really bad things happen that seem to come out of nowhere. No one saw it coming. It's as if a meteor fell out of the sky and landed on us. We were just in the wrong place at the wrong time.

Oh, really?

Behavioral scientists who study the human side of enterprise are hard to convince that anything we humans do, whether individually or in groups, is accidental. Behavior is not random. The complex and multiple causes of our behavior may not be apparent, but all behavioral events have causes.

Among the causes of some of the really bad things that happen in organizations is conflict. Let's look closer.

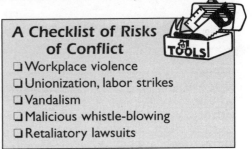

A Checklist of Risks of Conflict
❏ Workplace violence
❏ Unionization, labor strikes
❏ Vandalism
❏ Malicious whistle-blowing
❏ Retaliatory lawsuits

Workplace Violence

Daily newspaper headlines shock our sensibilities with acts of workplace violence. A disgruntled employee brings a gun to work to "settle the score" with a hated manager. A recently fired worker plants a bomb in the company's trash bin, killing several ex-coworkers, to "show them they made a mistake."

The National Institute for Occupational Safety and Health (NIOSH) reported that employees murdered over 100 bosses and coworkers in 1997. Homicide is the leading cause of death for women in the workplace and the second leading cause of death for men, according to the United States Department of Labor, Bureau of Statistics, 1995. According to Northwestern National Life Insurance Company, 2,500 workers per 100,000 have been physically attacked on the job.

Of course, psychologically healthy people do not commit acts of violence, no matter how much they may resent their workplace tormenters. So some form of psychopathology is a key cause of violence. But so is chronic interpersonal conflict that remained unresolved for a period of time prior to the violent act. Larry Chavez of Critical Incident Associates lists the absence of in-house employee conflict resolution systems as one of the organizational factors that contribute to workplace violence.

Security Threat
Workplace violence is the most important security threat to America's largest corporations, according to *Fortune* 1000 security executives surveyed by Pinkerton's Inc., as reported in its 6th annual survey, "Top Security Threats Facing Corporate America," released in March 1999.

Unionization, Labor Strikes

To be sure, organized labor and collective bargaining have played a vital role in the evolution of the improved workplace conditions and employee compensation that we enjoy today. We've come a long way since the 1930s and before, when workers had no protection against inhumane and sometimes brutal treatment by some corporations.

Just as surely, the formation of unions and strikes by workers are harmful to the fiscal health of companies and their shareholders.

So how can these events be prevented? Perhaps the best way to prevent unionization is to treat employees as if they were already unionized. That is, implement programs that address workers' needs before they conclude that the only way to get those needs addressed is to organize for adversarial action.

Happily, satisfying employees' needs is seldom simply a matter of paying higher wages or providing more expensive benefits. When non-adversarial methods of conflict resolution are used, many needs of employees can be met by non-monetary means. The expression, "Man does not live by bread alone," can be rephrased, "Employees do not work for money alone."

Studies repeatedly prove the obvious fact that chronic, unresolved conflict is a primary source of dissatisfaction at work. So, companies can often avoid the headaches of labor strife by managing conflicts effectively when they are informal clashes, before they escalate into formal disputes.

Vandalism

Examples from low-tech to high-tech ...

Case #1: A forklift operator employed by a Philadelphia shipping company once put his machine into low gear and left it running as he stepped off. The $35,000 piece of equipment crawled toward the end of the pier and dropped into the ocean. First explained as caused by carelessness, the incident was later investigated and the operator admitted that he had acted intentionally because he was angry with his supervisor for refusing to give him a requested day off.

Case #2: A computer programmer at a Silicon Valley company hacked into his company's system and altered the personnel records of a coworker that he disliked. The vandalism was discovered, but not before the coworker left the company for a position in a competing firm. She had not received a promotion that she was qualified for and probably would have received if her records had not been tampered with. The vandal later explained that the coworker "got on my nerves" and that his supervisor wouldn't do anything about her "offensive" behavior.

Were these acts of vandalism preventable? Certainly. These scenarios describe conflicts that are typical of those that can be readily resolved by using the mediation tools described in this book.

What if the forklift operator's supervisor had been able to use self-mediation to skillfully discuss the employee's desire for a day off and the company's staffing needs in a respectful and non-adversarial way? What if the computer programmer's supervisor had responded to the employee's early warning signs and used managerial mediation to explore a solution to the problem? Huge savings, in both financial and personal terms, could have resulted.

Malicious Whistle-Blowing

A shift supervisor at a nuclear power plant in Connecticut sent a letter to the Nuclear Regulatory Commission claiming that plant management was disregarding required safety measures, putting the plant at risk of a nuclear incident. NRC investigators regarded the claim as plausible and ordered the plan to shut down until the problem could be fully investigated. Three weeks later, it was determined that the plant was in full compliance with regulatory requirements and could resume operation. The cost to the utility company was over $3 million for each day it was out of operation.

Federal and state whistle-blower laws protect employees from company retaliation for alerting regulatory agencies of possible violations of requirements. Of course, public safety is served well by these laws.

But in the case of the Connecticut utility, the shift supervisor who blew the whistle had a history of unresolved disputes with management over a range of personnel issues, including compensation, promotion, and work schedules. Indeed, he was under review for possible job termination. But blowing the whistle to the Nuclear Regulatory Commission prevented any personnel action against him, at least until the complaint against the utility was resolved. The whistle-blower was a very intelligent and well-educated employee who knew how to use the law to his personal benefit. Indeed, his complaint was so expertly documented that it was never determined that it was a knowing-ly false claim. But people near the situation were quite sure it was a case of malicious whistle-blowing.

This incident cost the utility company over $60 million and disrupted electrical service to tens of thousands of residents in southern New England. Was it preventable? Probably so. If the ongoing conflict between the shift supervisor and his managers had been handled effectively, this huge cost could very likely have been avoided.

Retaliatory Lawsuits

The United States is perhaps the most litigious society in histo-ry. And our legal system is perhaps the most abused and mis-used part of the American system of government. Frivolous and retaliatory lawsuits, unlike those that seek compensation for damages caused by actual negligence, are increasing in both publicity and frequency.

Frivolous suits are those that are filed just because the plaintiff thinks there might be some money to be gained. Retaliatory suits are those that are filed because a grudging plaintiff hopes to inflict damage against the defendant and maybe make some bucks along the way. Good conflict-resolu-tion practices probably cannot prevent frivolous lawsuits, but they can prevent many retaliatory suits.

Managers and executives are particularly concerned about retaliatory suits filed by current or past employees, especially "wrongful termination" claims.

Here's an example. A clerical employee of a small munici-pality near Chicago opposed the city's planned budget-cutting measures. The employee spoke up angrily at public meetings of the city council, initiated a letter-writing campaign by citizens to city officials, and walked with a sign depicting the mayor as a devil in front of the city government office building. The employee's job performance had long been marginal, according to her department manager, and had recently deteriorated. Her manager claimed that she was increasingly uncooperative, sometimes belligerent, and unresponsive to the progressive discipline the manager applied. The employee won the suit, receiving over $200,000 in damages.

Was this simply a legal contest pitting individual free speech rights against employer rights? If the conflict between the employee and her manager had been managed better, might the city have avoided the need to divert $200,000 from other city services to pay the wrongful termination claim? Very likely so. "Progressive discipline" certainly has its place in the toolkit of human resource professionals. But discipline should not be applied before attempts to reconcile interests have been given a chance, except when criminal or ethical violations occur that cannot allow for compromise.

In the case of our Chicago suburb, there was no meaningful effort to discover the employee's underlying interests and to reconcile them with the needs of the municipal government. As a result, the employee was fired and proceeded to file and win a large damage claim, paid ultimately by taxpayers.

Hints to Avoid Conflict

There's no guaranteed way to avoid conflict. But you can do some things to minimize the negative consequences.

- Be sensitive to the relationships among your employees. Your job is not just to make sure the employees do their jobs, but also to be aware of *how* they do them.
- Encourage employees to come and talk with you. Don't take responsibility for resolving any conflicts, but do what you can to bring them out in the open.
- Analyze any conflict to determine the causes, both direct and indirect. The better you understand a conflict, the more effectively you can help resolve it.

According to your understanding of the conflict, choose and use one of the techniques presented in the following chapters of this book.

Detecting Submarines Before They Strike

The managers in charge in the illustrative scenarios we've just visited had no idea that the catastrophic events were about to happen. But was there no sign that a torpedo submarine was approaching? In every case, *someone* ignored information that could have led to action to avert disaster. Why did they ignore those signs?

Probably they just didn't know that there is a better way to resolve, manage, and even *prevent* workplace conflicts. They hadn't read this book!

Manager's Checklist for Chapter 2

❑ Conflict is not just an annoyance. It costs money—and those costs can be calculated, in terms of wasted time, bad decisions, lost employees, unnecessary restructuring, sabotage, theft, damage, lowered job motivation, lost work time, health costs, and legal expenses.

❑ Catastrophic events are usually the result of chronic unresolved conflict, which should have been noticed and properly managed.

❑ The costs and risks of conflict can be reduced by using the mediation tools described in this book.

How to Resolve
Any Conflict

We've been resolving conflicts for years ... *millions* of years. Indeed, our animal cousins resolve conflicts too. Did our ancestors read a book about how to do it? Do animals have a procedure manual to guide them? No. Resolving conflict comes naturally.

But resolving conflicts in a way that has positive outcomes for the disputants' relationship and for the organization or society of which they are a part does *not* come naturally. (Since this is a book about practical workplace mediation, and not an academic text, I'll not delve into the field of sociobiology, which studies cooperation, self-sacrifice, and altruism among animals.)

Conflicts among animals are essentially territorial or property disputes—you've got it and I want it. How do I get it? I use my power (superior physical size and strength, sharper claws, louder shriek) to try to overcome your opposition. If my power is sufficient, I win and get it. If my power is not sufficient, I lose and you keep it. That's also how conflicts were resolved among primitive humans: grunt loudly and carry a big stick.

Have we evolved? Well, yes and no. We're learning new and better ways to resolve our conflicts, but we're very far from being fully evolved, perfect beings.

The Three (and Only Three) Ways

Resolving territorial conflicts by using power is the most ancient way and still much practiced. But a few thousand years ago, when human societies became larger and more complex than a troop of a couple of dozen individuals who could be ruled by a single dominant leader, we needed to find a better way.

Some long-forgotten genius had an idea: Why not devise some rules about how conflicts *should* be resolved so when disputes arise we can simply refer to the rulebook, or to the leader who interprets the rules, to decide what the solution should be? That moment of creative genius was the big bang that produced our modern system of laws. That early thinker originated the revolutionary concept that individuals have *rights*. In theory, once individuals' rights are defined, conflicts can be resolved by determining whose rights prevail. But a swarm of flies eventually got into that ointment. Those early systems of rights, and today's civil justice system, still don't work perfectly.

Eons passed until the next conflict-resolution genius came along. In fact, only in the past couple of centuries—some would say only in the 20th century—did the next breakthrough occur. The idea gradually emerged that conflicts could be resolved by finding a solution that satisfies each disputant's interests.

Power contests and rights contests are similar in a key way: both are adversarial procedures. The main difference between them is the means used to win. In *power* contests, disputants use their resources (physical strength, credible threats, loud voice, number of allies) to coerce or intimidate opponents to comply with their demands. In *rights* contests, disputants appeal to a source of authority (parents, the boss, the policy manual, precedent, a court of law) to judge that their rights are more legitimate and therefore prevail over the rights of opponents. In both types of contests there's a winner and a loser.

But sometimes winners need for losers to be happy losers. The winner may need the loser to be voluntarily cooperative and trustworthy following the resolution of the dispute. That is, they continue to have an interdependent relationship. Simply vanquishing the opponent does not permanently solve the problem that gave rise to the conflict. Winning a battle does not end the war when you continue living or working with the enemy.

So, as society and organizations evolved over the past few centuries, people began to realize that power and rights contests have severe limitations when disputants remain interdependent after the resolution of a particular dispute.

Probably the first setting where this limitation became apparent was in families. Coercing or intimidating one's mate to comply with one's demands does little to provide an emotionally rewarding and supportive family relationship. The "winner's" needs for emotional support, safety, affection, and love remained unmet. And there's the ever-present risk of retaliation. (John Wayne Bobbitt, are you listening?) Long before anyone began using the terminology found in books about conflict resolution, husbands and wives no doubt realized that they needed to *negotiate.* That is, to get their own needs met, they each had to also find acceptable ways to meet the other's needs. Solutions had to be mutually consensual. Marriage, despite its reputation as a hotbed of hostility, was perhaps the birthplace of non-adversarial conflict resolution. When interdependency is intense, the need for consensus is great.

Businesses and other organizations have been rather late coming to this realization. Before the United States labor relations movement emerged in the early 20th century, companies typically viewed employees' labor as a resource to be exploited for maximum gain while paying as little for it as possible in wages, working conditions, and job security. When workers gained the legal right to organize—that is, to increase their power through collective action—company management was required to negotiate.

But, the word "negotiation" is used to refer to two very different processes: *power*-based negotiation (often called bargaining) and *interest*-based negotiation. The negotiation that goes on between organized labor and management is typically, and regrettably, bargaining. It is an adversarial power contest. Still, bargaining as a power contest is preferable over the alternatives—violence, strikes, and sabotage.

Few people, and fewer organizations, have discovered the remarkable benefits of interest-based negotiation, which is a *non*-adversarial process. Unfortunately, most people mistakenly think that being non-adversarial is being weak. They imagine that it involves caving in, giving up, conceding to the opponent. Far from it. Participating in non-adversarial dialogue is in our own enlightened self-interest—it's the best way to get our own needs met in ongoing interdependent relationships.

So, reconciliation of interests has emerged as a third way to resolve conflicts. The mediation tools you'll learn in this book will enable you to reconcile interests between disputing parties (including yourself) today so that voluntary cooperation tomorrow becomes possible.

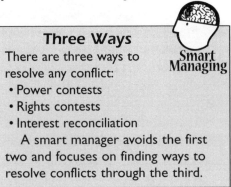

Three Ways

There are three ways to resolve any conflict:

- Power contests
- Rights contests
- Interest reconciliation

A smart manager avoids the first two and focuses on finding ways to resolve conflicts through the third.

Smart Managing

A Case: Modern Amalgamated Industries, Inc.

We see that, despite our advanced civilization and technological wizardry, our legacy as animals continues to set the pattern for how we manage our workplace conflicts even in the 21st century. Let's take a tour through a wild game park named Modern Amalgamated Industries, Inc. (MAI) and see how far we've come in resolving conflicts since the days when we used rocks and sticks.

Luther is the Production Manager of Square Widgets at MAI. He has a degree in engineering from Tech U. and has worked at MAI for 20 years. Consequently, he has deep product knowledge and lots of management experience.

Erin is the Production Manager of Round Widgets. She has an MBA in marketing from State U. and has worked at MAI for

15 years. Her experience has mostly been in marketing and other support services. She was recently promoted to Production Manager as a result of her strong performance in other areas and her broad knowledge of the business.

A conflict has arisen between Luther and Erin. Both the Square Widgets and Round Widgets production departments draw upon the services of the same pool of design engineers to develop upgrades. Having worked in the design engineering pool, Luther has kept good relations with several old friends there. Erin, having spent most of her career in the marketing department, does not have close connections with the folks in design engineering, but she has some old pals in marketing.

Senior management of MAI has determined that upgrades to both square and round widgets must be developed within the next three months if the firm is to stay competitive with other companies in its industry. In fact, the marketing department has already placed ads in trade magazines and consumer media based on the assumption that Luther and Erin can have their respective products ready to ship in 90 days.

Both Luther and Erin were surprised to learn of marketing's ad campaign. Ninety days would be a tight but doable schedule if they were developing only one product upgrade. But to complete two upgrades in the same period will severely strain design engineering's resources. To make matters worse, it's now November and many employees have already planned to take time off for the winter holidays.

So Luther and Erin are in direct competition for the services of design engineering to meet the requirements suddenly placed upon them. The two have clashed in the past, so both are apprehensive about this challenge. In fact, they've exchanged some sharp words. Recalling our discussion in Chapter 1 that distinguished "disagreement" from "conflict," we recognize this as a conflict.

Let's take a seat on a comfortable sofa in the corner of Luther's mind and watch the wheels turn as he thinks about what to do about this conflict.

Power Contests

Luther's first impulse is to view the situation as a win-lose conflict. That is, he assumes that either he or Erin—but not both— will succeed in getting enough support from design to get their upgrades completed by the deadline. With this perceptual frame around the picture (the "facts"), he's certain there simply isn't enough capacity in design to do both upgrades in time. So, he readies himself for battle.

Luther sees his close ties with old friends and colleagues in the Design Engineering department as his most potent weapon. So, he makes some friendly visits to their work area to schmooze and refresh those ties. He invites Brooke, the Chief Design Engineer, to lunch to catch

> **Frame** (noun) A perception of a conflict situation that causes the perceiver to make assumptions and interpretations about what is true about the conflict and about what solutions are possible.
>
> **Reframe** (verb) To change one's perception of a conflict situation so as to see new possibilities about what may be true about the conflict and about how it may be resolved.

up on what's going on in her department and to have a friendly chat about life in general. After warming up their friendship over lunch, Luther mentions the "goof" made by marketing in their premature advertising campaign. He asks Brooke if she can help him out by ensuring that enough design resources will be allocated to upgrading Square Widgets to make sure it gets done on time. Brooke is sympathetic to her old friend's dilemma and assures him that she'll do what she can. Luther feels good about the meeting, confident that Brooke will come through for him.

Meanwhile, Erin also has a "win-lose" frame. From her vantage point, it looks like either Squares or Rounds, but not both, are going to get the support needed to get the upgrade finished by the deadline. It's just not going to be possible for both Luther and her to come out of this situation looking good. That's obvious, right?

Hearing through the grapevine that Luther is schmoozing with his old pals in Design Engineering, Erin decides to pull her strings in Marketing. She invites her old friend Hayden, the Director of Marketing, to lunch to reminisce about their student days together at State U. She shares her excitement about the tremendous sales potential of Round Widgets and that "we really need to let the marketplace know that we're on the scene." She asks Hayden to give more prominent placement to ads for Rounds than for Squares. With this greater visibility of her product, she hopes that MAI's highly public commitment to Rounds will cause senior management to instruct Design Engineering to pour all resources necessary into completing the Rounds upgrade on time. After all, a public failure in the marketplace would make the company look very bad! That's obvious, right?

We see that both Luther and Erin are taking an adversarial approach to the situation. Their perceptual frames around the facts cause them to view their conflict as a win-lose situation. Holding this view of reality, it makes perfect sense to both that they must approach it as a power contest. (So, have we evolved much?) Each one has powerful weapons: Luther's social ties to Design Engineering and Erin's to Marketing. Both managers hope, by deploying their weapons to defeat the opponent and gain a victory, to win the resources necessary to complete his or her upgrade on schedule.

Who will "win" this power contest? Certainly not Modern Amalgamated Industries!

Rights Contests

MAI is an orderly system that has rules, regulations, policies, precedents, and a hierarchy of authority. As savvy managers, Luther and Erin both know how to use that system to try to win this contest.

Luther knows that Chief Design Engineer Brooke has received instructions from top management about the need to upgrade both Square and Round Widgets in the next three months. So, he composes a well-crafted memo to the VP of Operations making a compelling case that upgrading Square Widgets should receive preferential support "in case resources get stretched thin." He cites statistics that demonstrate Square's market share advantage over Rounds, its greater contribution to sales revenues, and the fact that Rounds were upgraded more recently than Squares, so "now it's our turn."

Also understanding how the system works, Erin writes an equally compelling memo citing other statistics: Rounds is an innovative "new technology" product, with a more promising future than the more traditional Squares; Rounds' market share is increasing while Squares' market share, although currently greater, is decreasing. Therefore, concludes Erin, "if tough resource allocation choices must be made, it is clearly in the interest of MAI to ensure that Rounds gets the support it needs to meet the deadline."

Arguments presented to third-party decision-makers, such as those posed by Luther and Erin, are essentially an appeal that "my rights are more legitimate than my opponent's rights." The third party has the authority to decide whose rights prevail. Statistics and other "facts" are persuasively presented in an effort to "win" the judgment. As Benjamin Disraeli remarked over a century ago, "There are three kinds of lies: lies, damn lies, and statistics."

The rights contest is institutionalized in American society, as well as in most other countries, as the legal system. Indeed, our judicial system explicitly uses the adversarial process, bound by rules of evidence and standardized procedures, to seek truth and justice. Judicial rights contests work admirably, although not perfectly, in settling criminal and many civil cases brought by plaintiffs against defendants. (Recall certain notorious and widely publicized trials in which common sense was sacrificed on the altar of judicial procedure.)

It's too bad our national obsession with rights contests has leaked—or flooded—into organizations, contaminating how we resolve daily workplace conflicts.

Who will win the rights contest between Luther and Erin? Perhaps one of them will. But their working relationship won't. And Modern Amalgamated Industries certainly won't!

When we resolve workplace conflicts by using tactics to defeat our opponents in power or rights contests, we may be victorious. But we win a Pyrrhic victory: we lose more than we gain. What will happen the next time Luther or Erin needs the other to provide functional or material support? If they hold grudges and sore feelings about having "lost" the contest between Squares and Rounds, they'll be unlikely to receive it. If they perceive—regardless of the reality—that the other used deceptive tactics, secret manipulation, and dirty tricks to win the contest, they will be even less likely to receive it.

Isn't there a better way?

Interest Reconciliation

Happily, there is a better way. And, that better way can be employed in nearly every instance where our perceptual frames cause us to see conflicts as win-lose situations, impelling us into power and rights contests.

Imagine that Luther, instead of framing the situation as a power or rights contest, viewed it as one that might be resolved collaboratively. With that frame around the "facts," he would go directly to Erin to communicate with her in a non-adversarial way about the impending problem. He would acknowledge that their respective departments appeared to be in competition for the same scarce resources (the services of the Design Engineering Department). He would express his hope that they could search together for a way to approach the problem that would benefit both of them as well as MAI. Erin, even if she were initially defensive and suspicious, would be disarmed by Luther's openness and candor and agree to join him in that search. She would recognize that her own interests would be best served by helping Luther and their company satisfy their interests as well.

Drawing upon both their friendly contacts in Design Engineering and in Marketing, they could devise a plan to enlist support from both departments in finding the best—or least bad—solution. As a team, they could jointly present their proposal to senior management, inviting executives' input and asking for their support.

Who would "win" under this scenario? Everyone. Luther and Erin would both optimize—not necessarily maximize—the resources devoted to upgrading their respective widgets. They would earn each other's voluntary support, trust, and generosity—a "good-will savings account" for future spending needs. Both would earn the respect of top management for working well together under challenging circumstances. And Modern Amalgamated Industries would have found the best solution to its production and marketing dilemma.

Interest reconciliation and collaboration is not weak—it's smart.

So, What Do You Really Want?

Conflict tends to divert our attention from our real interests by creating another interest—surviving or winning. That more basic, instinctive interest may eclipse your other interests and make it harder to resolve a conflict. So, just step back out of the conflict and away from anybody else involved in the conflict and think about what you would want if you could have a wish. That's your interest.

Simplify the situation. What do you *really* want?

Wrong Reflexes (Betrayed by Our Bodies)

OK, if taking a non-adversarial approach to reconciling interests is so marvelous, why don't we already do it? This concept isn't exactly rocket science! We don't have to be geniuses to comprehend the idea.

Indeed, the obstacle to resolving conflicts by reconciling interests is *not* a lack of intelligence. We already know a lot about conflict. Each of us has been studying it at the University of Life since the day of our birth. One thing we know very well is how to recognize it when it's happening. We are all experts at recognizing conflict.

Let's prove it. Jot down a list of 10 to 15 words and phrases that describe how you know that conflict is going on between other people. What behaviors do you see? What kinds of comments do you hear? What shows you that they are angry toward each other and not being friendly?

Chances are you came up with a list something like this:

Behavior Type A	Behavior Type B	Behavior Type C
Avoiding personal contact	Getting others to take sides	Sweaty palms
Writing memos instead of talking	Shouting	Nervous gestures
Withholding needed information	Pre-empting (getting there first)	Closed body posture
Not returning messages	Threatening	Tense facial expression
Delaying giving required support	Undermining the opponent's reputation	Crying

The composite of the three columns paints a picture of conflict as we know it. Even young children recognize that these behaviors mean that people are angry toward each other.

Now, think about what the behaviors within each of the three columns have in common. What category names would you give behavior types A, B, and C?

Most people quickly recognize that the column A behaviors are passive, the column B behaviors are aggressive, and the column C behaviors are unintentional. That is, the first two behavior types are *strategies* for handling a conflict situation and the third type is *non-strategic*—just the way our bodies involuntarily react under the stress of being in conflict.

These two strategies—popularly known as "flight" and "fight"—are the same two strategies that animals have used for millions of years to handle threatening situations. Recall that this chapter began with the comment that we've been resolving conflicts for millions of years. Well, this is how we've been doing it.

Do these strategies work? Yes, they work perfectly well—if domination and escape result in acceptable outcomes of conflicts. Indeed, this was the case for the many millions of years during which these behavioral reflexes evolved. Using them increased the likelihood of surviving life-threatening encounters with predators. They helped us survive another day, maybe long enough to produce offspring offspring whose genes contained instructions—"fight or flee, choose correctly and immediately"—for how to survive another day, and so on. That's natural selection in action.

But in the modern workplace, we deal daily with conflict in ongoing interdependent relationships in which domination

> **Instincts?** [!] CAUTION!
>
> Don't follow your initial instincts. Your first reaction is probably wrong.
>
> The "fight or flight" response is a physiological response to danger. It focuses us on what's wrong in a situation. A natural reaction that saved the lives of our ancestors is likely to hurt work relationships—and create more situations of danger.

and escape do not work. We have to work with people who behave in ways that we perceive as threats to our self-interests, yet whose trust and cooperation we must somehow gain. But our bodies are equipped by nature only with these two ancient reflexive tools for responding to those threats. They are *wrong reflexes.*

Have we evolved? Well, evolution clearly hasn't yet rid us of these ancient reflexes—and don't hold your breath waiting for them to atrophy from disuse.

Let's take a look at how our savvy and capable production managers, Luther and Erin, are playing out their wrong reflexes.

Distancing and Coercion (Walk-Aways and Power Plays)

The conflict between Luther and Erin began the moment they became aware of the scarce resource (support from Design Engineering). But the simple fact that there was a scarce resource that they both needed was not enough to cause their conflict. After all, two other people may have approached that factual situation in a cooperative

> **Key Term**
>
> **Distancing** The modern form of the "flight" reflex. Its purpose is to ensure our safety by avoiding contact with our adversaries.
>
> **Coercion** The modern form of the "fight" reflex. Its purpose is to ensure our safety by defeating our adversaries.

fashion. How they *framed* the facts is what created their conflict.

The perceptual frame around that simple fact that Luther and Erin used to interpret its meaning included ideas like:

- "We are in competition with each other, and competitions are to be won."
- "He/she will try to use those resources and prevent me from using them."
- "My career will be harmed if I lose this competition."
- "I can't trust him/her to care about how I am affected by the outcome of this, so I've got to do whatever's necessary to take care of myself."

These and similar interpretations are the *frame*—they are *not* the facts. They are inferences that these two individuals drew about their situation. Two other people in an identical situation may not have drawn those inferences. Why do Luther and Erin perceive the facts the way they do, rather than in some other way?

Their perceptions may be influenced by past experiences that have shown each of them that the other is a vicious competitor with a killer instinct. Their perceptions are also greatly influenced by their personalities, which are formed by their early childhood experiences mixed with their particular genetic predispositions.

Regardless of how they were formed, their perceptual frames cause Luther and Erin to employ adversarial tactics. But they are not helplessly predestined by their pasts and their personalities to frame conflicts as adversarial. Our pasts and our personalities *impel*, but they do not *compel*. We can't choose the *facts*, but we *can* choose the *frame*. Unfortunately, without some education about conflict, such as reading this book, our choice of frame is too often unconscious.

Given how Luther and Erin framed the facts, which in turn caused the conflict, how did they act? What behaviors did they employ in striving to win the contest?

Let's call the specific behaviors that illustrate the distancing reflex "walk-aways" and those that illustrate the coercion reflex "power plays." Luther and Erin avoided talking to each other (a walk-away). They each went to an old friend to get support (a power play). They wrote memos attempting to persuade executive decision-makers to give preferential treatment to their own department's needs (a power play).

Are these tactics so different from those employed by animals, or by our human ancestors, in trying to win territorial disputes? The playing field has changed—the corporate office instead of the jungle floor—but the game's the same.

It's bad enough that walk-aways and power plays are unnecessary and misguided tactics, arising from a option-limiting perceptual frame around the facts. But to make matters worse, these tactics by one person tend to provoke retaliatory walk-aways and power plays by the other person, which in turn elicit retaliatory walk-aways and power plays by the first person, and so on. This is how conflicts escalate.

Recalling our discussion of workplace violence in Chapter 2, every violent act is the culmination of a series of retaliatory exchanges of walk-aways and power plays that got out of control. And no one saw the torpedo submarine coming? Maybe no one recognized its tell-tale shadow—the series of escalating walk-aways and power plays—before it lurched abruptly and tragically to the surface.

A Better Way

Don't just sit there, crying in your beer about our innate inability to resolve conflict. True, our human heritage has equipped us with conflict-handling weapons that are more likely to cause self-inflicted wounds than to produce glorious and permanent victories. True, those weapons are more suitable for surviving life-and-death fights on the plateaus of Africa than for resolving personality clashes in the 15th floor conference room. But our human heritage also enables us to *think*. We can't *fight* our way out of conflict, but we can *think* our way out of it.

Let's dig deeper into this idea that conflicts may be

resolved by reconciling interests. How is that done? Each of the next three chapters will describe a mediation tool to use instead of our wrong reflexes. Let's preview what these three tools have in common.

First, there must be dialogue. Common sense and life experience tell us that if there is no dialogue, there can be no solution—that is, there can be no consensual, interest-based solution. And, as we have already established, that's the only kind of solution that works for managing our important, interdependent relationships. Solutions that result when one party imposes his or her will upon the other or when one or both parties withdraw from the relationship are not acceptable in the workplace: they incur costs and risks. We've got to keep working together and we've got to find solutions that each party will help implement. Anything less hurts the business. Anything less hurts us as people.

But what we need isn't just any kind of dialogue. The kind of dialogue that produces consensual solutions to conflicts is called "the essential process of mediation."

Second, the dialogue must be protected. Interruptions, distractions, and intrusions must be prevented. Imagine that the conversation is being held on the moon, completely isolated from the hustle and bustle of daily work life. The closer we can get to that ideal isolation, the better.

> **Key Term**
>
> **Essential process of mediation** Dialogue that is (1) directly between disputants, (2) limited by the cardinal rules, (3) about the issue to be resolved, (4) sustained long enough to find a solution.
>
> **Cardinal rules** Requirements for dialogue during mediation:
> 1. We must stay in the essential process—no walk-aways.
> 2. We must not impose one-sided solutions—no power plays.

Third, the dialogue must be given time. Time is the sacrifice we make to the gods that grant us success in mediation. It is the precious nonrenewable resource that we must expend to get value from interdependent relationships. Maybe sad, but certainly true.

The things we do to protect the dialogue and to

give it enough time are called "managing the context." Upcoming chapters will describe the kind of context needed for each mediation tool.

> **Context** The "time and place environment" in which dialogue takes place.
>
> *Key Term*

Fourth, the dialogue must be facilitated by someone who performs the "primary tasks" of the mediator.

So, we're learning how to think our way out of conflict. Wrap your mind around this kernel in the nutshell: to reach a consensual solution to a conflict, we must have a mediated dialogue in a managed context. The next three chapters will show how to do this to resolve three kinds (structures) of conflicts that every manager runs into: interpersonal conflicts between others, interpersonal conflicts between self and others, and team conflicts. Then, in Chapter 7 we'll look at how to apply our insights about mediation to prevent conflicts from arising at all.

> **Primary tasks** The behaviors that the mediator performs during dialogue (the essential process of mediation) that are necessary and usually sufficient to produce agreement.
>
> *Key Term*

Manager's Checklist for Chapter 3

❑ There are only three ways to resolve any conflict—by power contests, by rights contests, and by interest reconciliation.

❑ We are biologically ill-prepared to resolve conflicts. We tend to react in two ways: "flight" (distancing, walk-aways) and "fight" (coercion, power plays). But we can learn how to *think* our way out of conflicts.

❑ We can't choose the *facts* of a conflict situation, but we *can* choose the *frame*—our perception of the situation, our assumptions and interpretations.

❑ To reach a consensual solution to a conflict, we must have a mediated dialogue in a managed context.

How to Resolve a Conflict Between Others

Managers manage people. People are human. Our human nature impels us into conflict. So, managers must manage conflicts between people who work for them.

But you didn't need me to tell you that. Every manager, supervisor, team leader, and anyone else who is responsible for the work of others could write a book of case studies about conflict between employees—and most of their tales would not have happy endings.

Curiously, even the best graduate schools of business provide little or no instruction about how to manage the *relational* performance of employees. Sure, there are lots of academic courses and supervisor development programs for managing *individual* performance. But somehow the glaringly obvious fact that workers have relationships with other workers, and that therein often lies the rub, has been generally overlooked.

This is even more surprising since it's been estimated that over 60% of performance deficiencies result from problems in relationships, *not* from problems in individuals. Your own book of case studies would no doubt contain many laments about

it takes work to get alone

conflicts between employees who, individually, were skilled and capable workers, but who just couldn't seem to get along with each other. If so, this is your chapter!

A Case: Catastrophe Mutual Insurance Company

Eileen leads a team of seven program analysts at Catastrophe Mutual Insurance Company, headquartered in Kansas City. All team members are well qualified for their positions and the most recent new hire was over a year ago, so there's no problem with anyone's technical competencies or job knowledge.

The problem is an ongoing clash between Ty and Bea, two of the more experienced members of the team. Ty is very outspoken about his opposition to abortion, declaring that "any idiot can see that a human life is lost every time there's an abortion." Bea is equally vocal about her views in favor of abortion rights. She retorts, "You should get out more, Ty. You've got no idea what's in store for a pregnant teenager or for her baby. Who do you think you are to make her decision about whether to wait until she's older to start a family?" Ty suspects that Bea has had an abortion herself, which has blinded her with guilt to the fact that abortion is murder. Bea denies that she has had an abortion, but says her views would be the same even if she had. She says Ty is a right-wing wacko who is out of touch with real life.

Although the abortion issue is totally unrelated to the work that Eileen's team does, Ty's and Bea's contempt for the other's personal values creates a tense atmosphere. A highly publicized recent shooting in a family planning clinic in the Kansas City area sparked caustic exchanges between them. They try to avoid each other so they won't be taunted into a fight. As a result, they don't freely provide information that the other person needs for analyzing programs. Other members of the team try to stay uninvolved, but the tense atmosphere puts a damper on everyone.

Trying to quell the conflict, Eileen has told Ty and Bea to leave their opinions about abortion at home, since it has nothing to do with their work at Catastrophe Mutual. But somehow they find ways to tweak each other with subtle references to events in

Coping with Conflict

How much time do you spend dealing with employee conflicts?

A recent study reported that 42% of a manager's time is spent on reaching agreement with others when conflicts occur. What would you estimate as the percentage of your time that you spend on employee conflicts? More important, what percentage would be acceptable?

Source: Carol Watson and L. Richard Hoffman, "Managers as Negotiators: A Test of Power Versus Gender as Predictors of Feelings, Behavior, and Outcomes," *The Leadership Quarterly* 7 (1), 1996, 63-85.

the news or when casual conversations among team members drift toward politics and social issues.

Eileen is at her wits' end and is considering transferring both Ty and Bea out of her department. But she's afraid to lose their technical skills, knowing that replacements would probably be new hires who would require extensive one-on-one training.

Options

So what's a team leader to do? Eileen reviews her course notes for the MBA that she received a few years ago from Kansas Tech, but doesn't find much help. Her options seem to be limited to the following:

- *Ignore.* Sometimes conflicts go away if you ignore them—but more often they just get worse.
- *Threaten.* Sometimes people will "go along to get along" but more often they defy threats and become even less cooperative.
- *Separate.* Sometimes the amount of required interaction between disputing employees can be reduced by physically separating them or restructuring their job duties without impacting productivity. More often, however, efficiency and performance suffer when work is organized around the people, instead of people being organized around the work.
- *Terminate.* Getting rid of feuding employees completely resolves the conflict, but it can cost a lot to replace

them. (Recall our discussion of this cost factor in Chapter 2.) And, in the modern era of workers' rights, involuntary termination is not quite as easy as saying, "I divorce thee" three times.

- *Counsel.* Sometimes coaching employees individually can guide them out of the conflict. More often, the well-meaning manager-coach gets drawn into the problem by appearing to take sides, even if he or she intends to stay neutral, and then becomes someone's opponent—hardly a solution to the conflict.

Eileen despairs. She sees that these options offer little hope of helping Bea and Ty become voluntarily cooperative coworkers. What's worse, the downside risk of taking action may be even more serious than the consequences of doing nothing at all.

But wait! Don't despair! There's another option!

Managerial Mediation

A better way for Eileen to handle this problem is to act as an impartial third party to help Bea and Ty find a way to work together that they can accept and that also meets the needs of the company. But how does she proceed?

> ### Don't Go It Alone
>
> It's usually a good idea to discuss the pros and cons of your options with a human resources professional or other personnel expert. But don't assume that they know about all the options. Managerial mediation is still a new tool that many human relations experts don't know about yet.
>
> **Smart Managing**

Step 1: Decide to Mediate

Aside from considering her options, Eileen must take other factors into account. Every good decision is an informed decision. What information will assure her that deciding to mediate the conflict between Ty and Bea will be the right option?

Does the tool fit the problem? Eileen does a little research and finds out that the purpose of managerial mediation is defined as follows:

To reach and record a balanced, behaviorally specific, mutually acceptable agreement that defines each one's future behavior with regard to the business problem caused by their conflict.

Using mediation for the wrong purpose ensures failure and risks "killing the patient with the cure." What are some wrong purposes?

- To establish innocence and guilt. The appropriate process for finding out who is at fault for doing something wrong is investigation, not mediation.
- To discipline or punish. Using mediation for disciplinary or punitive reasons sends the wrong message. If an individual has violated legal or ethical requirements, then discipline may well be called for. But to discipline in the name of mediation inoculates employees against future use of mediation by giving them a bad experience with it.
- To decide right and wrong. Framing the conflict as one to be resolved by deciding who is right and who is wrong surely won't work. After all, mediation seeks *consensual* solutions—why would any disputant consent to a solution that defined him or her as the one who is wrong? Poetically speaking, not you, not me, not Ty, not Bea.

In short, mediation is a tool for *planning the future*, not judging the past. We can't change the past, but we can change the future.

Who defines the problem? If Eileen were to ask Ty and Bea what the conflict is about, they might actually agree on something. They might agree that the conflict is about whether abortion should be legal. But Eileen realizes that their opposing views about that volatile issue are not the business problem. As their team leader, she doesn't give a tinker's toot what Ty and Bea think about abortion. What she cares about is getting them to work together cooperatively as program analysts on her team.

Eileen as the manager decides *what* problem is to be solved by mediation. But she will let Bea and Ty decide *how* to solve it. Eileen will delegate to them the joint responsibility and authority for deciding how to solve the problem of their relational performance on the job.

So, managerial mediation is not a personal service for the benefit of the disputants. Rather, it is a business meeting to solve a business problem, specifically a business problem caused by the behavior of employees who are in conflict.

> **What's the Problem?**
> Listen to the conflicting employees' ideas about the situation. But don't leave it to them to define the problem to be solved by mediation. If it's unclear what the problem is, ask yourself, "Why does their behavior matter to me?" Your answer is probably a pretty good statement of the business problem caused by their conflict.

When should managerial mediation *not* be used? Some conflicts have causes that should be addressed primarily by other means, and maybe secondarily with mediation. Such as ...

Violations of legal or ethical requirements. Supervisor Pat has been making unwanted and persistent sexual innuendoes toward worker Dale, despite Dale's repeated statements of disinterest in Pat's overtures and requests that they cease. To which Pat replies, "Jeez, Dale, can't you take a joke? Loosen up!" Feeling increasingly uncomfortable with the situation, Dale finally goes to Pat's manager, Oliver, for help. Oliver has observed Pat's vaguely lascivious manner and has heard the occasional tasteless jokes, but he hadn't felt that Pat's dubious behavior had risen to the level of sexual harassment. He now thinks that maybe the line has been crossed.

What should Oliver do? Although there's clearly a conflict between Pat and Dale, which is causing a business problem, his first approach to solving it should probably not be mediation. Rather, the better tack would be a confidential discussion with Pat about appropriate workplace behavior. If the woodshed chat fails, stronger personnel action may be necessary. But if Pat's behavior is addressed and corrected and if tension remains between the two coworkers, Oliver might try mediation to help them repair the damage to their relationship.

not be used

Substandard individual job performance. Old-timer Matt and newcomer Morgan are lathe operators at Richmond Tool and Die, a precision machine shop. Over his many years in the trade, Matt has become highly skilled, and takes pride in his time-efficiency and in producing very little unusable scrap. Morgan recently completed a training program at Ray County Community College to become a certified machinist. Their supervisor, Megan, hired Morgan last month despite having concerns that he still had a lot to learn to do the high-precision work in her shop.

Tension has been rising between Matt and Morgan. Morgan makes a lot of mistakes, so sometimes Matt has to interrupt his work to correct the mistakes so that rush customer orders can be completed on time. Recently Matt has been heard shouting at Morgan, saying things like "if you can't run with the big dogs, get off the team."

What should Megan do? She recognizes that Morgan's performance is substandard and that his progress is slower than she hoped. Again, mediation may not be her best first approach. It would make more sense to give him additional training to bring his performance up to an acceptable standard, although it will probably still not reach Matt's level. While the training is under way, Megan could use managerial mediation with the two workers to get them to work more cooperatively.

not be used

Personal problems. Pam's job performance as a clerk at the Department of Redundancy Department, a government agency, has been declining for the past several months because she's been having a hard time lately. It all started when her husband, a truck driver, announced that he wanted a divorce. She had a drinking problem years ago, but has been sober since she became pregnant with her first child, now six years old. Newly single with three little kids, Pam is struggling emotionally and financially. Her ex-husband pays the required child support, but his truck driver salary isn't enough to keep her bills paid. Last month she moved to a smaller apartment to save money. Pam feels embarrassed about these problems and doesn't share details about her life with coworkers—especially with Clay, who works at the desk beside Pam's. Clay is getting increasingly impatient with Pam's moodiness and irritability. She snaps at him over little things like the noise he makes while chewing gum and scooting his chair on the floor. Typically easy-going, Clay is starting to bark back at Pam. Other employees who work within earshot of Pam and Clay are becoming annoyed by their sniping.

Her manager, Denise, has been watching this scenario unfold and deteriorate. She knows that Pam was recently divorced and thinks that may be the reason she's often late for work, particularly on Monday mornings. She is sympathetic to Pam and wants to be patient while she gets her life back in order, but she's also concerned about the impact of her personal problems on the important work done in the Department of Redundancy Department. It doesn't seem to be getting better.

What should Denise do? Clearly there's a conflict between Pam and Clay. Should she mediate? Probably not, at least not as her first course of action. Fortunately, their employer has an Employee Assistance Program (EAP). Denise reviews the booklet distributed by the EAP to all managers that explains how to refer employees for services. She understands that it's not her responsibility to investigate or diagnose the personal problems that may be causing Pam's performance to deteriorate. But it *is* her responsibility to talk with Pam about the necessity of satisfactorily performing her duties and to give Pam the EAP's toll-free number to call if she needs help in addressing any personal problems that may be causing her performance to decline. Then, once Denise has made the EAP referral,

Don't Diagnose! Managers should not attempt to diagnose an employee's personal problems, including alcoholism, that may be causing a performance problem. If you're unsure about how to hold a referral conversation with an employee, contact your company's employee assistance program or your human resources department for guidance.

managerial mediation may be helpful as a secondary tool.

Is it worth the time and trouble? Eileen's team at Catastrophe Mutual is understaffed and overworked. Time is at a premium. She knows that mediation requires at least an hour, often two, to be successful. Can she afford to take Ty and Bea away from their regular duties to have such a lengthy meeting?

She uses Chapter 2 of this book to estimate the financial cost of the conflict between her two employees. The resulting figure startles her! Once she lifts her jaw up from the floor, she decides that it's worth the investment of time in resolving their conflict so they can get back to productive teamwork.

Eileen now has no doubts: the return on investment of doing managerial mediation makes her decision a no-brainer. What's next?

Step 2: Hold Preliminary Meetings

Eileen first schedules a private meeting with Ty and a private meeting with Bea. In each of these two preliminary meetings, she wants to accomplish four things:

1. *To hear each person's side of the story.* Eileen opens each discussion with a comment like "I understand that you and Ty/Bea have not been getting along well lately. I'm concerned that your tension is interfering not only with your own work but also with others on the team. Tell me about the problem as you see it." She then listens to each employee's version of the situation, taking care not to agree or disagree with any criticisms either one may make about the other. She draws out more details with open-ended questions like "So, why do you think that is?," "Can you tell me more about that?," and "How does that affect you?"

Eileen understands that the purpose of inviting her employees to tell their own side of the story, without her coaching or advice, is not obvious. One might logically assume that the reason for asking questions is to hear the answers, so as to gain information about the problem. But Eileen recognizes that her role is to mediate, not to judge. She will not be using the information given by Ty and Bea to come up with a solution. She knows that when the three of them meet together, Bea and Ty may not be very good listeners and each may become frustrated by the other's refusal to accept the "obvious truth" of his or her own views (frames) of the problem. In their frustration, they may appeal to Eileen, the impartial mediator, to take sides.

By giving both employees an opportunity to fully tell their side of the story in advance and by conveying that she understands—not necessarily agrees with—their opinions and views, Eileen is laying the groundwork for a fruitful three-way meeting. Ironically, her hearing each employee's version of the problem helps to prepare *them*, not *her*, for the next day's three-way meeting.

2. *To define the business problem to be solved*. Recall that the manager-as-mediator decides *what* is to be solved; the disputants decide *how* to solve it. Unless the manager provides a clear definition of the business problem that makes the meeting necessary, the conflicting employees may try to solve the wrong problem. Here's what Eileen tells Bea and Ty in their separate preliminary meetings:

> Your views and feelings about abortion are your own business. They are not the business of this company. What *is* the business of this company is your job performance. Individually, each of you is a skilled, competent, valuable employee. But the difficulty that both of you are having in working cooperatively is impacting your own performance, and also that of your teammates. So, I want you two to figure out a way to conduct yourselves with each other so it doesn't have that negative impact.

Notice that Eileen is careful not to criticize either Ty or Bea personally, nor to make any judgment about who is at fault. Rather, she puts the focus on their *relational performance*.

3. *To explain key information about the three-way meeting*. Our human nature doesn't make it easy for us to grasp the idea that our authorities (people with power) can be impartial and nonjudgmental. We naturally expect leaders to act as

judges or arbiters who impose solutions, not as unbiased neutrals. (Recall the comparison of humans to animals discussed in Chapter 3.)

So, it's important that Eileen describe her neutral role to Bea and Ty. She explains, "I'll be there to help you two find a solution that works, but I won't be deciding what that solution should be. I'll be something like a traffic cop, just to help you talk to each other. It'll be up to you two to solve the problem. I probably won't by saying much while you do that."

Eileen also asks each employee to make arrangements to prevent any interruptions (cell phones, pagers, etc.) for at least 90 minutes as they talk to each other about the problem and how to solve it. If, and only if, she fears that either employee might become so angry that abusive or insulting language could occur, Eileen would remind them that they are expected to keep their discussion professional and businesslike and to behave respectfully toward each other.

4. *To secure their agreement to attend.* Recall the discussion in Chapter 3 about our natural, although counterproductive, wrong reflexes. The wrong reflex we named "distancing" can cause employees to try to avoid a face-to-face conversation with a detested coworker.

In Eileen's preliminary meeting with Ty, he says, "Eileen, I respect you as a team leader, but you just don't seem to understand. Bea is absolutely inflexible and irrational. There's no point in sitting us down to talk about this. It will only makes things worse. Frankly, I think you should sit her down and talk some sense into her head. Surely you can see that she's the one who's stirring up trouble! Just count me out and let me get back to work."

We established earlier that managerial mediation is "a business meeting to solve a business problem"—it's not a personal service to the employees. So, the conflicting employees don't have the choice to participate. Eileen has already determined that Ty and Bea's conflict is a relational performance problem, so both parties in the relationship must be involved in solving it.

Ideally, both employees would be eager to participate and optimistic about the outcome.

But clearly Ty is not on board. So, Eileen replies to him, "I understand your reluctance about this, Ty. But since you are part of the problem, you've got to

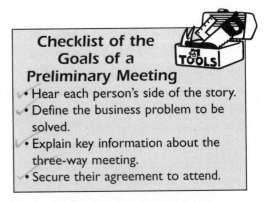

Checklist of the Goals of a Preliminary Meeting
- Hear each person's side of the story.
- Define the business problem to be solved.
- Explain key information about the three-way meeting.
- Secure their agreement to attend.

be part of the solution. So, I'd like for you to join me in the third floor conference room at 9:00 tomorrow morning. Consider it your job assignment to be there. I'll make sure that Bea is there too."

OK, Eileen has completed the preliminary meetings with Bea and Ty. In each meeting, she successfully accomplished all four purposes. Now what?

Step 3: Plan the Context

Now that Eileen has laid the groundwork with Ty and Bea and has scheduled a three-way meeting, she wants to prepare the time-and-place environment—the "context"—for that meeting. In Chapter 3 we defined the "essential process of mediation" as "dialogue that is (1) directly between disputants, (2) limited by the cardinal rules, (3) about the issue to be resolved, and (4) sustained long enough to find a solution." Eileen wants to ensure that the context will facilitate the essential process and that nothing in the context will interfere with that special kind of dialogue. She wants the setting to be as insulated from interruptions and distractions as if the meeting were being held on a distant planet. She thinks about the following aspects of the context:

Location. Having selected a conference room away from her team's regular work area, she has ensured that it will be *neutral* and *private.* "Neutral" means that the site is not home turf for either employee, so neither person is put at a psychological disadvantage. "Private" means that other people will not be watching, listening, or walking into their meeting.

Notice that Eileen chooses not to hold the three-way meeting in her own office, even though it would be neutral and could be made private. But meeting there might cause Ty and Bea to view her as an arbitrator instead of as a mediator. Arbitrators are neutrals who decide the solution. Mediators are neutrals who do not decide the solution. Although they may not have used the word to describe their role, most managers typically act as arbitrators—hence the phrase "management is the art of decision-making." The role of manager-as-mediator is uncommon. By selecting a location that does not imply her ordinary role of decision-maker, Eileen subtly reinforces the message to Ty and Bea that she's delegating decision-making authority to them.

Seating and physical surroundings. Eileen asks herself, "How can I use the tables, chairs, and other physical features of the conference room to help the essential process happen?" Common sense helps her answer the question. Having Ty and Bea sit across from each other at a sided table will help them keep eye contact and speak directly to each other. Sitting at the end of the table shows them that she is impartial yet in charge of the meeting. She understands that although she's delegating to them the authority to decide the solution, she remains in authority over the process of *how* the solution is decided. Hers is not a laissez-faire role.

For example, if Ty announced during the discussion that he thought nothing was being accomplished and he was returning to his desk or if Bea took offense at some comment by Ty and wanted to just walk out in protest, Eileen would remind them that they must keep going until they find a solution.

Eileen thinks about other aspects of the physical setting. She closes drapes to block the participants' view of distracting activities outside. She ensures that there are comfortable chairs of similar style. She arranges for a pitcher of water and drinking glasses so no one will need to leave the table to get a drink. She scans the environment for any other possible causes of distraction from the essential process.

Time of day, day of week. By selecting 9:00 as the meeting time, Eileen hopes that Ty's and Bea's mental energy and ability to actively engage in dialogue will be high. She has also thought about whether either employee might be distracted by any special events at work, such as making a key presentation to senior management or a planning a birthday party for a coworker. Her criterion for deciding time of day and time of week for the three-way meeting is simple and practical: "When will Bea and Ty be most able to focus their attention on resolving the conflict?"

Who is present? Eileen understands that managerial mediation is a simplification of professional mediation. (Recall our discussion of "self-help mediation" at the end of Chapter 1.) Using it does not require her to have received intensive training. Indeed, most people can successfully do managerial mediation by following the guidance in this book. So, she knows that managerial mediation is reliably effective when there are only two people in the dialogue. (To mediate multi-party, multi-lateral, and technically complex disputes, additional skills are needed.) Eileen has carefully defined the business problem so that only Bea and Ty are needed to solve it. (Chapter 6, How to Resolve Team Conflict, will describe how a team leader or group supervisor can mediate conflicts that cannot be defined so only two people can solve them.)

If Eileen's employees were members of a labor union and so had the contractual protection of a steward being present during disciplinary meetings, she would need to even more carefully explain that their three-way meeting is not a disciplinary process. Especially in unionized organizations with poor labor-management relations, it's often better to not use the term "mediation" when doing managerial mediation. Remember: it's just "a way to have a business meeting about a business problem." Employees who participate in managerial mediation often don't know that anything unusual is happening—except that their manager is not acting like a typical boss!

Length of time. Eileen has asked both Bea and Ty to make themselves available for at least 90 minutes. The key words here are "at least"—the managerial mediation meeting is *open-end.*

Managers are familiar with informational meetings, where the purpose is to exchange data, and with decision-making meetings, whose purpose is to identify and select options where decision-makers may have divergent opinions but are not in conflict. Those kinds of meetings usually should be *closed-end* events; that is, a time is set for concluding the meeting. This creates a sense of urgency and focus on covering the agenda before time runs out.

But Eileen understands that mediation is a unique kind of meeting. Rather than exchanging information or making a decision, mediation entails producing an *attitude change.* Specifically, Ty's and Bea's attitudes must change from "me-against-you" to "us-against-the-problem." (This is called the "breakthrough," which will be described a little later in this chapter.) The bad news is that the mediator can't just schedule the moment of mutual attitude change. The good news is that it usually happens within 90 minutes, assuming the essential process is maintained and the context was well planned.

So, managerial mediation is an *open-end* event; there's no ending time set. But Eileen is confident that Bea and Ty will change their attitudes within the time she's allotted. And she knows that once that breakthrough happens, solving the business problem will happen quickly. After all, interpersonal conflicts are not technically difficult problems to solve; the primary challenge is getting disputants to become *willing* to agree. Managerial mediation meets that challenge.

OK, Eileen has anticipated everything in the context for her upcoming meeting with Ty and Bea that might interfere with the essential process. What's next?

Step 4: Hold a Three-Way Meeting

It's now 9:00 a.m. the following day. Eileen arrives in the conference room a few minutes early to place chairs where she wants Ty and Bea to sit, to close the drapes to block their view of the company parking lot, and to place a pitcher of water and glasses on the table.

Bea arrives first. Eileen gestures for her to take one of the chairs on the longer side of the table. They make small talk for a few minutes until Ty arrives, chatting about the weather or other superficial topics that are unrelated to their meeting. Eileen remains standing, away from the table, so that when Ty walks in, he will clearly see that she and Bea haven't started without him.

Once they are seated and settled, Eileen begins:

Bea, Ty, thanks for joining me this morning. As you both know, I had a chance yesterday to hear your views of the problem that we're here to solve. Again, the problem is the impact on your own and others' productivity caused by how you interact with each other. We're not here to discuss your views about abortion. We're here to discuss how you can work together more cooperatively.

I've asked you both to clear your calendars for at least an hour and a half so we'll have all the time we need to solve that problem. Have you made arrangements to not be interrupted until we're finished here? (She pauses for both to confirm that they have done so.) Good. Thanks for doing that.

As I explained to each of you yesterday, I'll be kind of a traffic cop for your conversation. I may not say much at all. And I won't be deciding the solution—any solution that can work will have to be your solution.

Finally, we're here to find a solution—we're not here to find fault. Both of you may have strong feelings about this matter and I hope you'll express them openly and in a professional and respectful way. I'll help you stay on the path toward a solution.

Any questions? (She pauses for any procedural questions.) OK, then, who'd like to start?

After she makes her opening comments that create a constructive and positive frame for the three-way meeting, Eileen sits back in her chair to listen and watch. For what?

Her antennae are tuned to pick up two signals:

Departures from the essential process. Do Bea and Ty stay on the topic of the business problem, which is how they interact with each other at work? Or do they lapse into an argument about abortion? Or do they talk about safe but irrelevant subjects, like weather and sports, or even tell jokes? Or do they become hopeless about the likelihood of success in the meeting, hoping instead to be excused from this unpleasant and stressful situation? Or do they stop talking entirely, lapsing into obstinate silence? Or do they try to get Eileen to take sides by persuading her to agree with their opinions?

When she sees that either Ty or Bea is trying to disengage from the essential process, Eileen gently and firmly nudges them back to it. She may respond with comments like the following:

> "How is what you are talking about related to the problem we're here to solve?"
> "I see that you're discouraged about this meeting. But let's keep talking."
> "Please talk to her/him, not to me."
> "My opinion doesn't matter here. You two need to find a solution that you can both agree to."

Conciliatory gestures. These are magical little creatures that scurry about in the dense undergrowth of interpersonal conflict, often unnoticed. They seem magical because of how powerfully they can affect the course of an adversarial argument, despite being so small and seemingly insignificant. They go unnoticed because they are often just a short string of words nested within a long defensive, combative statement.

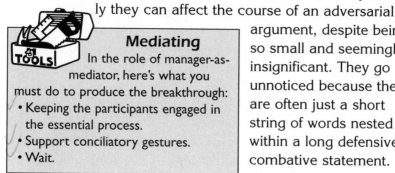

Mediating

In the role of manager-as-mediator, here's what you must do to produce the breakthrough:

- Keeping the participants engaged in the essential process.
- Support conciliatory gestures.
- Wait.

Here's an example:

A half-hour or so into the meeting, Bea says, "You know, Ty, you think you're so damn smart! You truly are a whiz as an analyst, and I could really use your help a lot of times. But when you look right at me when you say words like 'immoral' and 'selfish' and 'babies,' it just sets me off. I know you're just trying to pick a fight. How can you be so narrow-minded?" Ty immediately reacts: "Me, narrow-minded? How ridiculous can you be? Wow, talk about the pot calling the kettle black!" The argument continues.

But wait! Eileen noticed something. She interrupts their argument to say, "Bea, a moment ago you complimented Ty for being a whiz as an analyst and said that you could use his help. Can you say more about that?"

> **Key Term**
>
> **Conciliatory gestures**
> Verbal statements or parts of statements made during mediation that expose the speaker's vulnerability to exploitation by the other.

Bea's short remark, nearly hidden within her long angry statement, was a conciliatory gesture. But, because simply complimenting Ty would make her feel vulnerable to his gloating, she felt compelled to disguise it with a hefty covering of hostility. Doing so protected her from the possibility that he would take her compliment without giving anything in return. That would mean he "won one" on her mental scorecard.

With her sensitive antennae, Eileen heard the conciliatory part of Bea's comment and brought it out of the undergrowth and into the light of day. She invited Bea to say more about it, hoping that pointing to the unnoticed conciliatory gesture might spark a reciprocal gesture from Ty.

It didn't work this time; they kept arguing. Often,

> **Tools**
>
> **Being Conciliatory**
> Here's a list of kinds of conciliatory gestures:
> • Apologizing
> • Owning responsibility
> • Conceding
> • Self-disclosing
> • Expressing positive feelings for the other
> • Initiating a both-gain approach to the problem

Key Term Breakthrough The moment during mediation when there is a reciprocal exchange of conciliatory gestures, signaling the disputants' mutual shift in attitude from me-against-you to us-against-the-problem.

mediators must patiently wait for several conciliatory gestures, responding supportively to each one, before an exchange of gestures happens. When there are reciprocal conciliatory gestures, we have reached the moment of "breakthrough."

As Ty and Bea argue, Eileen is attentive to these two signals—departures from the essential process and signs of conciliation. They are two of the three primary tasks of the manager-as-mediator. But it's the third primary task that is often the most challenging part of mediating.

The third task is to *be quiet!* That is, to refrain from saying and doing any of the many things that common sense may lead us to think would be helpful:

- Don't give advice or suggestions.
- Don't propose ideas for solutions.
- Don't probe with "why" questions.
- Don't give your own opinions, even if the participants ask for them.
- Don't take "cool off" breaks.

What else do you think might be helpful? Don't do it!

So, managerial mediation is remarkably simple to understand, but it may be difficult to do since it requires that we stifle some strong impulses. Simply put, the manager-as-mediator keeps two questions in mind:

1. Are the participants in the essential process? If yes, do nothing. If no, guide them back to it.
2. Did either participant make a conciliatory gesture that the other ignored? If no, do nothing. If yes, give it your attention by pointing to the comment (because even the person who made it may not be aware of doing so) and asking the person who made the gesture to say more about it.

Focus on both of these two things and do nothing else. OK? Your mental concentration may be hard to sustain, but it's necessary for managerial mediation to work.

Eventually, the essential process leads to a breakthrough, which opens a window of opportunity for solving the business problem. Remember: solving the business problem is the easy part. Getting the participants *ready* to solve it, by shifting their attitudes from adversarial to cooperative, is the hard part—at least the part that takes patience.

Let's Make a Deal

When that window of opportunity opens, the manager-as-mediator seizes the opportunity to help the participants make a deal. Their deal describes how they will interact in the future to prevent the problems of the past from recurring.

So, what's a deal? What do you want to take away from the mediation table?

First, the deal must be *balanced*. That is, each employee must see a personal benefit from making the deal work, even though he or she may have had to make concessions or accommodations to the

> **Key Term**
>
> **Good deal** An agreement describing how the parties will interact in the future that is:
> • Balanced
> • Behaviorally specific
> • Written

other. It must pass the WIIFM test—"what's in it for me?"

Second, the deal must be *behaviorally specific*. That is, it defines in clear detail who is to do what, by when, for how long, under what conditions, with what assistance, etc. Vague agreements like "We'll try to get along better" are unlikely to stick.

Finally, it should be *recorded*. That is, notes are taken about the details of the deal. Ordinarily, these notes are written by the mediator, who then confirms with the participants that the deal accurately captures what they've agreed to.

Chances are, Ty and Bea will agree to refrain from making comments that are in any way related to the abortion issue in the presence of the other. They may contrive some creative features of the deal. For example, they may ask Sam, a coworker whom they both like and trust, to help out. Sam will serve as their monitor, giving the two-handed "T" signal for "time out" whenever Sam senses that a taunting tweak has occurred or he sees them coming too close to a fight. They may also agree to schedule a 10-minute "weekly tweaks" meeting every Friday afternoon at 4:00 for the next six weeks to share their experience of working together over the past week. Any resentments that come up are to be stored until the next meeting. After six weeks, if there are no more tweaks, the weekly tweaks meeting can be discontinued.

While Ty and Bea are creatively planning their solution, Eileen guides them to ensure that their deal is balanced and specific and she jots down some notes about it. When the deal is completed, she reads her notes to them to make sure it's accurate and acceptable to both employees.

After both participants accept the deal, Eileen expects them to comply with it. Ty and Bea are not free to simply abandon the deal if they don't feel like doing what they agreed to. After all, the company has invested time and other resources in this business meeting and consequently can expect its employees to follow through responsibly.

Whew! Eileen is relieved that Ty and Bea have made a deal. Is she done? Not quite.

Step 5: Follow Up

Before adjourning the meeting, Eileen proposes a time for Bea and Ty to meet in her office in a week or two. She clarifies that the purpose of this follow-up is not to have another meeting of the same kind as they've just completed. Rather, it is to review the deal and check on how it's working. She is *supervising their relational performance.*

Too Simple?

Sound simple? Sound *too* simple? If so, you are in the company of many learners of managerial mediation who at first doubted that such a simple tool can have lasting beneficial results in solving what have seemed like irresolvable conflicts. If you've got the time, I refer you to my description of the behavioral science of simple mediation in the book, *Managing Differences: How to Build Better Relationships at Work and Home.*

But you don't need to understand the theory to make it work. Do you understand the physics of fuel ignition, which makes your car run? Not me! But we all use its power to get us where we need to go. We can also use the power of the essential process of mediation in a planned context to move us from conflict to cooperation.

So, take your new vehicle for a spin!

Manager's Checklist for Chapter 4

❑ Managers have several options for dealing with an employee conflict. But mediation is a unique option because it produces voluntary cooperation, not just compliance.

❑ Most managers have the behavioral skills needed to mediate, but may not know how and when to use them. Managerial mediation is a template within which you can apply your current skills, once you understand the tool.

❑ Managerial mediation is conceptually simple, but may be hard in practice because we must stifle some impulses and overcome some misdirected common sense about how to help people in conflict come to agreement.

How to Resolve a Conflict Between Yourself and Another

I n the previous chapter, we learned how to resolve a conflict between two people by using simple mediation. Managerial mediation is about as simple as mediation can get, right? After all, performing the three primary tasks of the manager-as-mediator requires only that we use social and interpersonal skills that we've all learned during our decades of study at the University of Life.

But what if the conflict is between you and another person? What if your manager doesn't see what's going on, or doesn't care, or doesn't know what to do about it? In any case, you might rather handle it yourself without your manager getting involved.

In fact, that's the way it is about 99% of the time. That is, workplace conflicts that measurably damage productivity, performance, and profitability usually are *not* mediated by a manager or anyone else who takes initiative to resolve them.

What do you do then?

This chapter explains how to do "self-mediation." Do it yourself. Wear two hats. Negotiate in support of your own interests *and* do what a third-party mediator would do *if* a third-party mediator were present. It's an even simpler kind of mediation—"mediation without a mediator."

A Case: Hard Core Manufacturing, Inc.

Jay is production supervisor of the nuts division of Hard Core, a small company near Detroit that serves the automobile industry. Tarin is production supervisor of the bolts division. Jay and Tarin must work closely together, since their products must form a very tight fit.

Each division has about 20 skilled-trades employees who usually work in two shifts—day and evening. Sometimes a third shift (night) is necessary when the major auto manufacturers place large special orders for nuts and bolts. All 40 employees work in a large open area.

Hard Core's major customer, Simmons Motorcar, has had great success with the Woodstock, its sports utility vehicle designed for aging baby boomers. Simmons has redesigned next year's model of the Woodstock so bolts are screwed into threaded holes in the frame, not requiring nuts. Anticipating a large increase in orders for the Woodstock, Simmons has contracted with Hard Core to supply 30% more bolts for the next year and 30% fewer nuts.

This means that Tarin's division will face larger demand and Jay's work will decrease. Hard Core's owner and president, Mark, wants to ensure that the company successfully responds to this change, since Simmons accounts for about 60% of Hard Core's total revenue. Mark has instructed Jay and Tarin to reallocate resources between their divisions to achieve a smooth transition. The changeover will happen 30 days from now.

For the past several days Tarin has been walking around the factory floor watching nutters (employees who make nuts) on the job. She wants to select the best nutters so they can be retrained as bolters (guess what they make!) and transferred to her division. Cross-training and reallocating skilled nutters to be bolters would allow Hard Core to maintain the required output in two shifts.

Jay takes a different view. He believes that the 30% reduction in nuts orders from Simmons can be easily made up with new contracts with other automobile manufacturers and with companies outside the auto industry. Indeed, Jay has given the names of some contacts in other companies to Corwin, Hard Core's sales manager. Jay is active in the Detroit Chamber of Commerce and meets lots of business people at Chamber meetings. Instead of losing his skilled nutters, he thinks Tarin should hire and train new bolters to work a third shift.

The frame that both Jay and Tarin are putting on their situation creates a conflict. Both view it as a win-lose scenario in which their individual interests are threatened by the actions or perceived intentions of the other. Jay is at risk of his division being reduced, which would affect his personal income from Hard Core's profit-sharing plan. Too, he fears that he would wind up being perceived as Tarin's "little brother" if his responsibilities are lessened. Tarin sees the situation as an opportunity for greater income and influence in the company and doesn't want to miss this opportunity. So, her opinion is that it's impractical to hire new workers and train them as skilled bolters, since it's very hard to find good employees who are willing to work third shift. Both supervisors are using various walk-aways and power plays (remember the "wrong reflexes" discussed in Chapter 4?) as their positions polarize and their conflict intensifies.

Mark doesn't spend much time in the factory, preferring to schmooze with other executives on the golf links at Motor City Country Club. He's unaware of the growing conflict between Jay and Tarin. Frankly, they're glad he's not around. They like their autonomy in running their divisions and don't want Mark to interfere with the problem that's developing.

So what can be done about the impending catastrophe as Jay and Tarin become decreasingly cooperative in meeting the challenge posed by the new contract with Simmons, their very best customer? Will they screw up and lose the customer that gives them 60% of their business?

Jay picks up a copy of this book while browsing at a local bookstore. He does a quick calculation of the cost of the conflict and is shocked when he adds up the figures. His naïve assumption that he can "win" the conflict with Tarin, without inflicting harm upon himself, evaporates. He suddenly sees that light at the end of the tunnel for what it really is—an inbound train.

Jay reads the chapter about managerial mediation and wonders whether he should give this book to Mark and suggest that he mediate the situation. For several reasons, he's a little uncomfortable with that option. If the truth be known, both he and Tarin have little respect for Mark, who inherited the business from his family and who seems to view it simply as a cash cow to support his expensive golf habit.

As Jay reads further, he gets to the chapter about "self-mediation"—the same one you're reading right now. "Hmmm . . . ," he muses. "Maybe I can handle this situation myself, without Mark even getting involved!" So, what does this chapter encourage him to do about his deepening and potentially costly conflict with Tarin?

Self-Mediation

Managerial mediation and self-mediation have much in common beneath the surface. Jay flips back to the discussion in Chapter 1 about structure. He sees that both mediation tools are designed to resolve structurally simple conflicts. His conflict with Tarin is structurally simple: two interdependent people who, although they represent constituencies, have high negotiator authority and can talk to each other "same time, same place." And, he recognizes that, although their conflict is very important, it is not urgent—the changeover won't happen for a month, so there's time to talk together to avoid the train wreck. The structure of their conflict is suitable for both managerial mediation and self-mediation.

The key difference between these two mediation tools lies in who takes the initiative to resolve the conflict—their manager or one of the parties involved in the conflict? In those situations when, for whatever reasons, there is no third-party mediator, how does a person who is personally involved in a conflict use mediation to help resolve it?

We'll go through the process in four steps.

Step 1. Find a Time to Talk

Jay understands that an interest-based consensual solution to conflict cannot be reached without dialogue. So, the first thing he must do is find a time to talk with Tarin about the issue to be settled. He is careful to approach her at a time when they can have a few minutes of privacy.

The day after reading this chapter, Jay notices Tarin at her desk casually leafing through *Nuts Today,* a trade magazine. Since she's not too busy at the moment, this might be a good time to approach her. Jay says, "Hi, Tarin, do you have a minute? (The Approach)

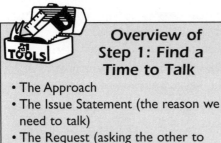

Overview of Step 1: Find a Time to Talk

• The Approach
• The Issue Statement (the reason we need to talk)
• The Request (asking the other to meet)
• The Sale (?)
• The Cardinal Rules (?)
• The Time and Place

"I've been thinking about how we should handle this changeover for the Simmons nuts and bolts order that's coming up. I'm getting concerned that we might be shooting ourselves in the foot by the way we've been dealing with it. Maybe we should put our heads together and figure out a solution that would work for both of our divisions and also for Hard Core. (The Issue Statement)

"I'd like for us to get together—just you and me—and talk about how we might work together on this. How about it?" (The Request)

Ideally, Tarin would welcome Jay's overture and agree that a conversation would be a good idea. Indeed, many organizations make it an explicit policy, and a performance issue, that any request by a coworker to communicate about a workplace problem must never be declined. Unfortunately, Hard Core Manufacturing is not so progressive. Tarin, who frames the situation as competitive and adversarial, is suspicious and skeptical.

She says, "I'm too busy to talk about that. I've got to finish up selecting the best nutters to be retrained as bolters."

In terms familiar to professional salespeople, Tarin—the "prospect"—has posed an "objection" to Jay's "offer." Jay must successfully counter the objection to make the "sale"—that is, to get Tarin to agree to meet to discuss a cooperative solution to the changeover problem. The general formula for countering objections is:

- *Acknowledge the objection.* Don't treat the prospect's reasons for declining your offer as unimportant or illegitimate. Recognize that within the perceptual frame of the prospect, his or her objection is a good reason not to accept the offer.

- *Show benefits.* Use the prospect's objection to point out how his or her own interests would actually be served by accepting the offer. If the objection is "I don't have time," show the time-saving advantages of your offer. If the objection is "It's not that important," show how the risks of not accepting the offer could be serious. If the objection is "We already talked about it and it didn't work," show that you've learned of a new approach that may yield success if the two of you try again to talk it out.

- *Ask again.* Repeat the offer. Sales professionals tell us that the single greatest reason that sales are lost is the salesperson's failure to ask again.

Jay skillfully counters Tarin's objections and finally gets her to agree to join him to discuss how to work together to achieve a successful changeover.

But Jay isn't quite finished yet with finding a time to talk. He understands that the meeting that he's setting up will surely fail if either of the two cardinal rules (remember them from Chapter 4?) is violated. So, he wants to shore up his confidence that their dialogue will not be wrecked by Tarin's either walking out of the meeting or imposing a one-sided, nonconsensual solution.

But Jay also understands that if he mentions the cardinal rules to Tarin, without giving some factual reason for his concerns, she could perceive that as an unwarranted accusation. He doesn't want to risk making her defensive, which could cause her to refuse to meet; he would then "lose the sale." He wants to "give peace a chance," to quote the song lyric by Beatle John Lennon.

So, Jay says, "Tarin, we could go on treating this situation as a competition between us, where one would win and the other would lose. But I suggest we spend as much time as necessary to listen to each other's ideas, trying the find a solution that's good for our own divisions and also good for Hard Core. So, I hope we can keep talking and exchanging ideas for a long while if necessary until we discover the best solution. It might get frustrating, but I'll agree to not give up the search for an hour or even two, if needed. Can you do the same?"

Finally, Jay wants to settle on a time and place for their conversation (The Time and Place). Appreciating that Tarin might be feeling a little manipulated by Jay's initiative in proposing a meeting, he invites her to suggest a time and place that's convenient for her. As long as it's a suitable context, free from interruptions and distractions, and a time that he can also meet, Jay is glad to offer Tarin this choice.

Notice that if no selling is necessary and if the initiator (the self-mediator) is confident that there's no risk of either cardinal rule being violated, finding a time to talk can be a *very* short conversation. It could take less than a minute to approach a coworker, state the issue, ask him or her to join you for a conversation about it, and decide on a time and place.

> ### Fools Rush in ....
> **Smart Managing** While finding a time to talk, take care not to get drawn into a discussion or argument about the issue. In this step, we just need to *label* the issue, not *resolve* it.
> Remember: this is only a conversation about having a conversation—it's not the conversation itself.

Step 2. Plan the Context

In addition to selecting, with Tarin's input, a time and place for their discussion, Jay attends to many of the same particulars about the setting for their upcoming dialogue that Eileen thought about as she planned her three-way meeting in managerial mediation. Most simply, he wants to prevent interruptions and distractions.

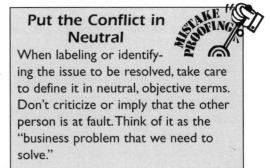

Put the Conflict in Neutral

When labeling or identifying the issue to be resolved, take care to define it in neutral, objective terms. Don't criticize or imply that the other person is at fault. Think of it as the "business problem that we need to solve."

Step 3. Talk It Out

The "talk it out" step of self-mediation resembles the "three-way meeting" step of managerial mediation. In both, the *essential process of mediation* (remember this from the last chapter?) is necessary for success—sustained dialogue between Jay and Tarin about the issue. "Finding a time to talk" and "planning the context" are preparatory steps to help ensure that the essential process will happen.

Context Checklist

- ☑ Where?
- ☑ Private
- ☑ No phones
- ☑ No walk-ins
- ☑ When?
- ☑ Enough time?
- ☐ No scheduling conflicts
- ☐ Too tired?
- ☐ Physical comforts
- ☑ Seating
- ☑ Noise
- ☐ Temperature
- ☐ Liquids

Tarin and Jay decided to meet in the company's conference room, which is adjacent to Mark's office and some distance from the shop floor. (Don't worry about interference from Mark; he's at the U.S. Open golf tournament.) They each have asked an experienced employee in their divisions to be temporarily in charge of operations, so they won't be interrupted. Jay buys a couple of soft drinks from the vending machine in the lunch room, remembering to get Tarin her favorite flavor—a thoughtful courtesy to set a positive mood. They exchange small talk as they sit down at the conference table.

Once they are settled, Jay starts the discussion:

"Tarin, thanks for joining me for this conversation. I know

meeting

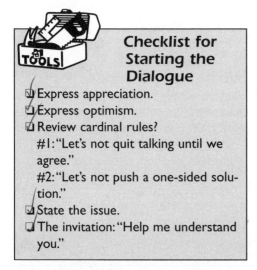

Checklist for Starting the Dialogue

☑ Express appreciation.
☑ Express optimism.
☑ Review cardinal rules?
    #1: "Let's not quit talking until we agree."
    #2: "Let's not push a one-sided solution."
☑ State the issue.
☑ The invitation: "Help me understand you."

you weren't very enthusiastic about it and I appreciate your taking time for this during a very busy period for you. (Expresses appreciation.)

"I also understand that you have your doubts about whether we can find a way to work together in planning the changeover that will turn out better for you than the way we've been going about it. I'm pretty sure we can do that if we put our heads together and think creatively. (Expresses optimism.)

"So we are both committed to giving this a try, right? We'll keep up the search for at least an hour or so, even if it gets frustrating, for a plan that we both feel OK about before either of us resorts to doing anything on our own without the other's approval? (Reminds Tarin of cardinal rule #2. Notice that Jay doesn't mention #1, since he isn't concerned that Tarin will walk out of the meeting. She's never done it before, so there's no reason to ask her not to do it now.)

"OK, my understanding of what we're hoping to work out in this meeting is a way to reallocate resources, possibly including employees, between our two departments so that Hard Core can produce the nuts and bolts that Simmons Motorcar will need for its new model of the Woodstock. Is that your understanding? (States the issue.)

"Maybe a good place to start is for you to help me understand exactly how you see the situation. What do you think we should do and why?" (The invitation.)

Jay's opening comments take less than a minute. He ends by inviting Tarin to tell him how she sees the situation. That invitation launches the dialogue.

The dialogue could take a couple of hours. What happens

during that time? What does Jay do?

Jay wears two hats—a negotiator hat and a mediator hat. He plays two distinct roles in this meeting.

As a negotiator, he is trying to get his own interests satisfied. He needs to

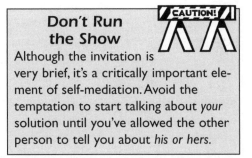

Don't Run the Show

Although the invitation is very brief, it's a critically important element of self-mediation. Avoid the temptation to start talking about *your* solution until you've allowed the other person to tell you about *his or hers.*

preserve his status as a production supervisor of equal standing with Tarin. He needs to prevent loss of financial income as an employee of Hard Core, including his profit-sharing revenue. He needs to maintain good relations with Tarin and with Mark because he knows he will need them in the future.

How does Jay negotiate to get those needs met? Well, he'll negotiate without even knowing that he's negotiating—because you can't *not* negotiate! We are all negotiating all the time we are interacting with others who have or control things we need. We negotiate with our coworkers as we decide where to go for lunch (we need their companionship at lunch *and* we need to eat food that we like). We negotiate with our employees as we try to get them to do their jobs effectively (we need their productivity *and* we need to minimize the time spent supervising them). We even negotiate with our spouses as we discuss how to decorate the family room (we need them to be happy with the results, since an unhappy spouse does not a happy marriage make, *and* we *too* need to be happy with the results).

We are dependent upon other people to give us things we need. And we need to maintain good relations with our coworkers, our employees, and our spouses because we know we'll also need things from them in the future. Negotiation is the process by which we get other people to give us the things we need while also trying to maintain good relations so we can get more things from them in the future.

(Does this sound cynical? Selfish? Self-centered? At first, maybe so. If we took the time to examine the self-serving func-

Don't Go to Extremes

Smart Managing Be *assertive* while negotiating—not *passive* and not *aggressive*. That means we try to get our needs met without depriving others of getting their needs met. When we are passive, we don't try at all or we give up too soon. It is our *human right* to have our needs considered and respected, even if they can't always be fully satisfied. Assertively protect your right—but don't violate the other's right by being aggressive!

tion that's imbedded in acts of altruism, generosity, self-sacrifice, and even love, you might put a less negative frame on selfishness. But that's a subject for another book!)

In any case, Jay isn't feeling very generous toward Tarin right now. He's scared about losing status and income if she gets her way and turns his best nutters into bolters. And he's angry about how she's been behaving lately. So, he negotiates with his own interests foremost in his mind.

If Jay were an expert negotiator, he could negotiate better with Tarin. But he's not. His negotiation skills are unpolished. He argues. He interrupts. He raises his voice. He's rude.

Does this mean his attempt to self-mediate fails? Not necessarily. If the essential process is allowed to continue unabated for a sufficient time, self-mediation usually works. That is, issue-focused dialogue that is protected from interruptions and from fatal violations of the cardinal rules still produces conciliatory gestures, just as it does in managerial mediation.

What is Jay doing in his other hat—the mediator hat? While he's negotiating for his own interests, how is he playing his role as mediator?

Remember what Eileen did as a third-party mediator? She had three primary tasks:

1. Keep the essential process going.
2. Support conciliatory gestures.
3. Patiently wait for the breakthrough.

Jay does much the same. He makes sure that neither he nor Tarin gives up, quits, or changes the subject to safer but irrelevant topics. And he listens for conciliatory gestures in Tarin's comments. Of course, he also offers them himself when he can do so sincerely. But he can't insist that Tarin reciprocate his own conciliatory gestures. He can only "give peace a chance" by offering and supporting conciliatory gestures. Voluntary cooperation is just that—voluntary. Peace can't be forced. (That's why the United Nations troops who are deployed in trouble spots around the world are called "peace*keepers*," not "peace*makers*.")

As their discussion continues, Jay and Tarin argue heatedly about what should be done.

Jay says, "Tarin, stop trying to steal my best nutters. I've invested a lot of time in training them and you can't have them. They're *mine!*"

Tarin counters, "Jay, you're just being selfish. It's obvious that the best solution is to put the best employees where they are needed most. With the new Simmons contract, that's in *my* division! You may not like it, but that's the truth. Get used to it!"

So far, their conversation isn't looking very promising. This frustrating, discouraging argument may go on and on. Jay even tries to offer constructive suggestions, but Tarin ignores them. He's

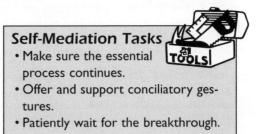

Self-Mediation Tasks
• Make sure the essential process continues.
• Offer and support conciliatory gestures.
• Patiently wait for the breakthrough.

starting to think he made a mistake in setting up this meeting.

But wait! Listen! After a while, the tone of the conversation changes.

Tarin says, "You know, a friend of mine manages production at Screwnuts Corporation, a company like ours not far from here. He told me the other day that their biggest customer, Horseless Steamcars, is going out of business so they'll be laying off some nutters. Maybe I could take a look over there. But I'm still going to need your best nutters to quickly cross-train as bolters. I've got to be in full production the day after the changeover. Any idiot can see that!"

Did you recognize the conciliatory gesture in Tarin's comment? Jay did! He heard Tarin make a concession, retreating from her previous position that all the nutters she'd need for the changeover must come from Jay's division.

Before reading this book, Jay might have reacted like this: "Look, Tarin, you can't have a single damn nutter from my shop! They're mine and you can't have them! And by the way, don't call me an idiot, you idiot!"

But instead of reacting defensively, Jay seized the opportunity presented by Tarin's conciliatory gesture: "Tarin, I appreciate your flexibility about looking for other sources for good bolters. Maybe I could help you evaluate the skills of the nutters being laid off at Screwnuts, to help you select the best ones. I understand that your division will be a pressure cooker when the changeover happens. Also, if I could get a couple of good workers from Screwnuts, we could transfer a few of my best workers to your side of the shop. I'll take the time to train the nutters from Screwnuts to get them up to speed so they'll meet our higher quality standards."

Smart Managing

Accentuate the Positive, Ignore the Negative

Skilled self-mediators understand that conciliatory gestures are often mixed with more hostile comments. It's best to disregard the aggressive words and tone, to focus instead on the conciliatory. How? Acknowledge the gesture, show your appreciation of it, and reciprocate. Seize this window of opportunity to make a deal before it slams shut.

Step 4. Make a Deal

This exchange between Jay and Tarin was the "breakthrough"—the same kind of breakthrough we defined in Chapter 4: "A mutual shift in attitude from me-against-you to us-against-the-problem." Once the attitude shift happens, the two supervisors can approach solving the problem with a "both gain" assumption about possible outcomes of the conflict. Until that moment, they assumed that the only possible outcome was win-lose or, even worse, lose-lose.

Happily, now that both Jay and Tarin view a both-gain outcome as being possible, they proceed to make a deal—the same kind of deal that we saw Bea and Ty make in Chapter 4 with Eileen's third-party mediation: 1) balanced, 2) specific, and 3) recorded. They work out a plan for interviewing and selecting the five best nutters being laid off from Screwnuts. They agree that those new hires will replace five of the most skilled nutters in Jay's division, who will be quickly retrained as bolters and transferred to Tarin's division. They agree to work with sales manager Corwin to draw on Jay's contacts in the Chamber of Commerce to develop new customers. This new business will compensate for the loss of the Simmons business for Hard Core's nuts division so Jay's responsibilities won't be reduced. Finally, they agree to meet jointly with Mark when he returns from the U.S. Open golf tournament next week to share with him their plan for a successful changeover.

> **Key Term**
>
> **Win-lose** "If I win, then you lose" (and vice versa). A win-lose assumption implies that only a "winner take all" outcome is possible.
>
> **Lose-lose** "If I lose, I'm going to make sure you lose too." A lose-lose assumption implies that losing is inevitable, which is palatable only if the other also loses. So, the other must be prevented from winning ("I'll take you down with me").
>
> **Both-gain** (commonly called "win-win"): "I believe each of us can benefit." A both-gain assumption allows a non-adversarial search for common ground to serve the common good.

Some readers of this book will be able to reframe *all* conflicts as having potential both-gain outcomes. Those lucky few will have successfully escaped from the perceptual trap that produces win-lose and lose-lose assumptions. Using the mediation tools described in these chapters, they will be capable of managing differences without conflict in all their important relationships. They will have eliminated conflict from their lives.

Jay, although he read this chapter before meeting with Tarin, had not transcended ordinary human limitations to reach such

Wisdom of the Ages
Rumi, the Persian poet, wrote 800 years ago, "Out beyond ideas of wrongdoing and rightdoing there is a field. I'll meet you there." Wiser counsel has not been heard since.

an exalted plane of peace. But he used self-mediation well enough to succeed in reaching an agreement with her. Once he learns to use preventive mediation, described in Chapter 7, he may achieve enlightenment.

Manager's Checklist for Chapter 5

❏ The necessary functions of a third-party mediator can be performed by people who are personally involved in the conflict, if the conflict has a simple structure and if the people can balance the two roles of negotiator and mediator.

❏ Self-mediation resembles managerial mediation. The primary difference between the two dialogue tools lies in who initiates the process of resolving the conflict.

❏ Frame conflicts as *both-gain* opportunities instead of *win-lose* or *lose-lose* contests.

How to Resolve Team Conflict

So far we have learned how to use mediation tools for resolving conflicts having simple structures—two interdependent individuals who do not represent constituencies and who are able to communicate at the same time in the same place. Happily, most business problems caused by workplace conflicts can be defined, if caught early enough, so that managerial mediation and self-mediation can resolve them. After all, nearly every conflict starts with two people.

But into the life of every manager falls rain that misses that bucket. Sometimes conflicts cause problems that require more than two self-representing players to resolve.

A Case: The General Case Study Company

The General Case Study Company (GCSC) is a small firm in the San Francisco Bay Area that produces instructional case studies for use in adult-learning settings ranging from college MBA courses to corporate training programs. Each case contains three parts: the "story," which portrays a problematic situation; the "analysis," which describes how to understand the problem by using concepts and theories of the subject matter being studied; and the "proposal," which recommends a course of action for solving the problem that is based on the analysis.

These three parts correspond to the stages of expert solution of other kinds of problems, including medical ones. For example, when you visit your physician, he or she asks questions about your symptoms and performs tests (the "story"), diagnoses your problem using his or her expert medical knowledge (the "analysis"), and decides upon a treatment plan (the "proposal").

Being a matrix organization, GCSC is composed of several production teams, each one consisting of five people: a storyteller, an analyst, a proposer, and a quality checker, all under the guidance of a team leader. The storyteller writes a journalistic report of a problem that is appropriate to the subject matter being studied. The analyst analyzes the story using expert knowledge of that subject matter. The proposer proposes how the protagonist or other character in the story should use subject matter expertise to solve the analyzed problem. Finally, the quality checker ensures that the three sections of the case study fit together to form a well-written and realistic teaching aid.

Each specialist (storyteller, analyst, and proposer) reports to the functional manager who oversees production of that part of the finished case study. Specialists are hired on a project basis to fulfill specific customer contracts, whereas functional managers, team leaders, quality checkers, and senior executives are permanent employees and stockholders in the company.

The subject matter to be taught with the case studies that GCSC produces range widely from management to marketing to communication to business operations. The company can produce case studies for learning virtually any subject matter. GCSC's customers are often college deans and department chairs who need case studies for use in their classrooms. Publishing companies also contract with GCSC to produce cases for textbooks.

Two months ago GCSC received a contract to write 50 cases on the subject of workplace mediation for Mediationworks

Press, Inc., the major publisher in its field. GCSC's production manager, Shawna, immediately began recruiting 12 qualified specialists to assign to three production teams. Within a few weeks, she succeeded in finding talented storytellers, analysts, and proposers who had knowledge of workplace mediation and who were available to work on this 90-day contract.

Shawna's team contains the three functional managers, Abby (Manager of Storytelling), Bob (Manager of Analysis), and Kristine (Manager of Proposals). Also on her team are the three project team leaders, Madison, Melissa, and Sarah. David, the Quality Manager who supervises the quality checkers assigned to each team, completes Shawna's management team of seven people.

A conflict on Shawna's team has already arisen, less than a month into the Mediationworks project. Only two of the first nine cases submitted to the customer were accepted. The others failed to meet the explicit quality criteria that Mediationworks provided at the start of the contract. This early failure places in jeopardy the completion of the required 50 cases within the three-month contract period. The contract also allows for financial penalties if more than half of cases submitted fail to meet Mediationworks' strict quality criteria.

Members of the team are naturally pointing a finger at David and his quality checkers. But David replies, "Look, I was just trying to give you folks a break. Is this the thanks I get? The quality was so poor coming out of the teams that I tried to cut a few corners to give your specialists time to get up to speed, and Mediationworks snagged us. Bob, your analysts are especially weak. They just don't seem to know much about workplace mediation."

Bob, in defense of his analysts, retorts, "Hey, don't blame my people. They're as good as anyone in the field and I've trained them thoroughly. The problem here is that the stories that Abby's people are coming up with are implausible. They sound fictional, and Mediationworks told us the cases need to be highly realistic."

Now it's Abby's turn to react. "Hey, back off! My people are writing good stories—we spent the first several days brainstorming some very realistic workplace conflicts. You team leaders are just not coordinating the three parts of the cases well enough."

We get the picture. The team has encountered failure and no one wants to be blamed. Not only is there a business problem to solve (rejection of cases by the customer), but there is also a conflict to resolve.

Recall our definition of conflict in Chapter 1: interdependent people who feel angry and find fault, and whose behavior causes a business problem. The finger-pointing at each other is compounding the business problem by wasting the human resources needed to perform the work. (Review the cost factors we discussed in Chapter 2 to estimate the resources wasted because of this team conflict.)

How does the structure of the conflict that Shawna faces at GCSC differ from the structure of the conflicts that Eileen resolved with managerial mediation at Catastrophe Mutual Insurance and that Jay resolved with self-mediation at Hard Core Manufacturing? The key structural difference is the number of parties. Clearly, the conflict on Shawna's team is not reducible to an interpersonal clash between two people. Also, some of her team members represent constituencies—the contract specialists who tell stories, analyze, and propose. But the team members have high negotiator authority: they have the power to make a give-and-take deal with little need to check with their temporary employees to make sure the gives and takes are OK. Fortunately, like Eileen and Jay, Shawna can bring the people involved in the conflict together at the same time and in the same place to have a dialogue.

How can Shawna resolve the conflict on her team so the members can effectively apply their talents to producing satisfactory cases for Mediationworks Press?

Team Mediation

Managerial mediation and self-mediation require very little skill of the mediator, whether the mediator is a neutral third party or

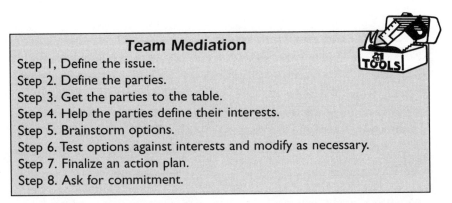

Team Mediation

Step 1, Define the issue.

Step 2. Define the parties.

Step 3. Get the parties to the table.

Step 4. Help the parties define their interests.

Step 5. Brainstorm options.

Step 6. Test options against interests and modify as necessary.

Step 7. Finalize an action plan.

Step 8. Ask for commitment.

one of the disputants wearing the two hats of mediator and negotiator. In both kinds of mediation, the breakthrough that signals that the disputants are ready to solve the problem happens spontaneously, without sophisticated interventions by the mediator. Conflicts with simple structures can be resolved quickly and simply, without much skill by the mediator.

When conflict happens on teams or in groups, that is, when the conflict structure is more complex, the mediator can't rely so heavily on the natural process that is imbedded in human nature that spontaneously produces breakthrough. Team mediation is a bit more complicated. More skill is required of the team leader-as-mediator than of the manager-as-mediator and the self-as-mediator.

Step 1. Define the Issue

Shawna sits at her desk, doodling with a pad and pencil, wondering aloud. "What's the problem that I need to solve? What's the *issue*—the matter of concern to GCSC? Is it that David's quality checkers failed? Is it that Bob's analysts didn't produce technically accurate analyses? Is it that Abby's storytellers didn't write realistic stories? Is it that my team leaders failed to coordinate the functions of all specialists?"

She quickly realizes that each of these possible definitions of the issue is flawed. Each one places blame. Each one assumes that the weak link in the chain of sequential tasks is already known. Each one focuses on the past, not on the future.

She doodles, "GCSC is not meeting our customer's expectations." That sounds a bit better, but still seems too focused on past failure. She reaches over to a bookshelf for her tattered copy of this book—the very one you are reading now—and thumbs back to Chapter 1: What's a Conflict? Her eyes settle on the scenario of Susan and Sean, the teammates who disagreed about how to solve a technically difficult problem. Their disagreement was not a conflict, since they were able to listen to each other's ideas and consider their merits. This helps Shawna realize that her team's conflict is not simply a lack of consensus about how to meet Mediationworks' requirements. Finally, she writes in big block letters, "How can we cooperate to meet our customer's expectations?" She feels comfy with that definition of the problem. "*That's* the conflict that must be resolved to solve the business problem," she concludes. "*That's* the matter of concern to GCSC. *That's* the issue."

Step 2. Define the Parties

Next, Shawna considers who should be included in the dialogue to resolve that conflict. Should the 12 contract specialists be included, along with her seven full-timers? That's a large number, which could make the meeting unwieldy. Moreover, the team leaders and functional managers have enough negotiator authority to represent the interests of their specialists. Should she include senior executives? The top execs are not operationally involved in producing cases. As production manager, Shawna has the authority to solve problems that arise in her area of control. So, she decides against including the big bosses. Should she include every functional manager and team leader? Yes, she decides. Each of them has ideas to contribute

Create Clusters

When a large number of people need to be included in team mediation, natural clusters or sub-teams may be formed consisting of individuals with similar interests at stake in resolving the conflict. Each cluster should select a spokesperson who reports to the full team. Breakout rooms may be used to allow clusters to reach consensus in private before reporting to the full team. Facilitators or co-mediators may be needed to help clusters perform their discussion tasks and reach consensus during breakouts.

and, even more important, each one has to buy into the solution and be committed to implementing it.

Step 3. Get the Parties to the Table

Shawna sends an email inviting the seven individuals to the meeting, making sure the complete distribution list is visible to each recipient, so everyone knows who else is being included. She states the issue to be resolved: *How we can work cooperatively as a team to meet Mediationworks' requirements?* She states that she has arranged an off-site venue for their meeting, 8:00 a.m. to noon next Wednesday morning, and asks all members to ensure they won't be interrupted by phone calls or pages. She also mentions in her email that she'll personally visit with each recipient in advance to discuss any questions he or she may have about the upcoming meeting.

Create a Safe Environment

Smart Managing

When multiple levels of hierarchy are included in team mediation, the mediator may need to coach senior members in advance about the need to assure junior members that they won't be harmed by being candid in disclosing their thoughts and feelings during the mediation. Junior members may need to hear that reassurance directly from senior members. Hopefully, that reassurance will be sincere and its sincerity will be trusted. Fear of retaliation, whether founded or unfounded, undermines the success of mediation.

When Shawna makes her rounds to visit each member of the team, most of them welcome the opportunity to gather to figure out how all can pull in the same direction. David, however, is reluctant. "I know what's going to happen," he declares. "It's just going to be a 'bash Quality' party. Everyone has already decided that my checkers and I are at fault for the early failures. I don't want to

CAUTION!

Keep It All Out in the Open

Openness and transparency is important. Team leaders who are perceived by members as having hidden agendas, as keeping secrets, as playing favorites among members, and as using mediation as a deceptive manipulation for self-serving purposes are unlikely to succeed.

be lunch for that feeding frenzy, thank you very much. Count me out."

Knowing that it's essential for David to participate and ultimately to commit to a joint action plan, Shawna clarifies that the meeting's purpose is to find a plan for future action that all can fully consent to, not to cast blame on anyone for what's happened in the past. "We're there to find a solution, not to find fault," she assures him. But David is unconvinced and continues to object to the meeting. Finally, seeing that his mind won't be changed by her assurances, Shawna says, "David, I hear clearly that you prefer not to participate. But since you're a player in the problem, you've got to be a player in the solution. My job is to solve this problem and I need your help. So, please be there on Wednesday. Do I have your commitment to that?" Although David isn't Shawna's direct subordinate, he understands the politics of matrix organizations. She's made him an offer he can't refuse.

Although she would have liked for every team member to be eager to participate, Shawna is satisfied that all the necessary people will be present to participate in the process of solving the problem.

Step 4. Help the Parties Define Their Interests

It's now 8:00 in the morning on Wednesday. The off-site facility has provided a light continental breakfast and all members of Shawna's team are present. She asks everyone to take a seat around the conference table and she takes her place at the head.

She opens the meeting by posting on the wall a sheet of flipchart paper with the issue statement: "How we can work cooperatively as a team to meet Mediationworks' requirements?" Shawna invites any questions to clarify the purpose of the gathering. She's done a good job of explaining its purpose in step 3 (getting the parties to the table), so everyone is clearly aware of why they are all here.

"I think it's important that we all understand what's at stake—for ourselves and for each of the others on the team—in how we decide to resolve this issue," Shawna begins. "So, I'd like for each of you to share with the rest of us what matters to you about issue and how it gets resolved. I'll take notes on the flipchart."

> ### The Write Stuff: What's Right for You
>
> Many team leaders prefer to use an assistant, a "scribe," to write information on the flipchart, instead of doing it themselves. Some people are able to talk and write at the same time—others can't. Work within your abilities.

As each individual takes a turn responding to her "What's at stake for you?" question, Shawna starts a fresh sheet on the flipchart with that person's name and job function at the top—Abby: Storytelling Manager, Madison: Team Leader, and so on. On each sheet she records their replies—"To get information from others in a timely manner," "To not be blamed unfairly for problems that I and my workers didn't cause," "To not have my reputation tarnished by failures by others," "To not be yelled at," and so on. When their responses seem ambiguous or superficial, Shawna asks clarifying questions: "Why is that of special importance to you?," "Why does that matter so much to you?," "Tell me more about what that means to you," and so on, to dig beneath surface interests to more fundamental ones. Once each individual's interests are defined and recorded on a separate sheet of flipchart paper, she tears it from the pad and tapes on the wall for all to see.

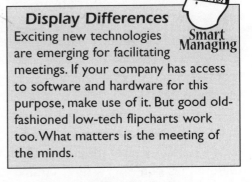

> ### Display Differences
>
> Exciting new technologies are emerging for facilitating meetings. If your company has access to software and hardware for this purpose, make use of it. But good old-fashioned low-tech flipcharts work too. What matters is the meeting of the minds.

Shawna reminds the group that they may alter their interest statements later in the meeting if new ones come to mind or if the initial wording needs to be clarified and sharpened.

When it's David's turn to describe his interests, he says, "To not be labeled as the 'bad boy' on the team." Shawna seizes this opportunity to allow some controlled ventilation of feelings:

"David, tell me about your perception of being labeled that way. What's that like for you?" She invites him to express his feelings and his views, but discourages him from blaming or criticizing others. Recall the distinction between "assertive" and "aggressive" that we clarified in Chapter 5. Shawna coaches David and others to be assertive without being aggressive.

After all members of the team have had a chance to articulate their interests, Shawna asks, "So do I understand correctly that if we can find a solution to the issue at hand that satisfies all these interests, then we will have solved the problem?" If they have all stated their interests well, they will all answer her affirmatively.

Let's take a moment to think about why Shawna is devoting time to drawing out the underlying interests of each team member. Her purpose is dual.

On a superficial level, individuals' interests on display—whether posted on paper sheets around the room or on a screen—serve as the criteria against which possible solutions will be tested later in the meeting. (More about that in coming pages.)

On a deeper level, enabling and encouraging each person to express his or her own ideas, opinions, views, and needs achieves the requirement of *differentiation,* which must precede *integration.* That is, during the mediation process—whether the conflict being mediated is interpersonal or group or intergroup or international—people must be allowed space to express their differences, to establish their identity as different from others, to talk about *me,* to assert *my* needs, to declare *my* values and opinions. Only after they have sufficient time to declare their differences can angry, fault-finding disputants become emotionally ready to consider their similarities and to integrate their interests into a common solution. That's human nature.

How does the shift from differentiation to integration happen in managerial mediation and self-mediation? What did Eileen and Jay do to accomplish this shift? In conflicts with simple structure, that attitude shift, which we named the "breakthrough," happens natural- ly and spontaneously. In Eileen's managerial media- tion, differentiation was partly achieved in the pre- liminary meetings, in which she listened non- judgmentally as Bea and Ty told their stories. In Jay's self-mediation, differ- entiation was partly achieved when he invited

> **Differentiation** The first phase of every mediation, which allows disputants to express and articulate their differ- ences. Sufficient differentiation paves the way for integration.
>
> **Integration** The second phase of every mediation, in which disputants are able to integrate their divergent interests into a common solution. Successful integration requires suffi- cient differentiation.

Tarin to begin speaking and then when he listened as well as he was able. Other than that, the mediator didn't have to do any- thing to make the breakthrough happen, other than keep the essential process going on long enough.

But, because the structure of team conflict is more complex, the mediator must actively manage differentiation among team members, allowing and encouraging assertive expression. The mediator ensures that it is balanced and non-inflammatory, not letting self-expression degenerate into a destructive shouting match. The structured activity that Shawna is using to elicit each person's underlying interests achieves constructive differentiation.

Preventing More Problems

To avoid problems, mediators of team conflicts should pre- vent the following three behaviors:

- *Personalization:* Don't allow people to use inflammatory personal insults and other derogatory language. Show your disapproval promptly when it happens.
- *Withdrawal:* Don't allow individuals to remain passive for a long peri- od of time. Each person needs to express himself or herself throughout the mediation process. Ask specific questions of with- drawn individuals to elicit their responses.
- *Scapegoating:* Don't allow subgroups to "gang up" on individuals or smaller subgroups. Encourage *individual* expression; discourage sub- group coalitions that lead to "us against them" power and rights contests.

Step 5. Brainstorm Options

Shawna has succeeded in giving space to every team member to voice their individual interests, which now paper the walls of their meeting room. She's ready to begin developing options for how the team members can work more cooperatively to meet Mediationworks' requirements.

Since her team is small, only seven members, she's fairly confident that everyone will speak freely and openly. But she harbors some lingering doubt about David and a couple of others whose body language raises concern. They are slouched in their chairs, arms crossed, as if to say, "I'll just watch and wait to see what happens here." Shawna knows that every individual must contribute to the solution. The "watchers and waiters" are like snipers hiding in the bushes, ready to shoot down others' ideas.

So, Shawna uses a form of the "nominal group technique" (NGT), first described by André L. Delbecq, Andrew H. Van de Ven, and David H. Gustafson in 1975 (*Group Techniques for Program Planning: A Guide to Nominal Group and Delphi Processes*, Middleton, WI: Green Briar Press).

First, she asks each team member to individually jot down at least three ideas, preferably more, in response to the issue

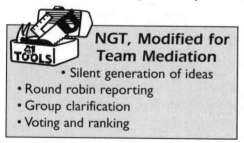

NGT, Modified for Team Mediation

• Silent generation of ideas
• Round robin reporting
• Group clarification
• Voting and ranking

question, "How can we work cooperatively to meet Meditationworks' requirements?" She allows three or four minutes of silence for them to do this. By having each person silently generate ideas, she ensures that every member will have input to the solution.

Second, starting with the person immediately to her left (or any other arbitrary position around the table), Shawna asks each member to report one of his or her ideas. She writes each one on the flipchart, building a growing list. She encourages people to continue to think of new ideas as the "round robin" reporting proceeds, adding them to their lists. Whenever a member has run out of items to contribute, he or she passes. Reporting continues until everyone has passed, indicating that no one has any more ideas. By gathering ideas in this manner, Shawna ensures that no one member dominates. And by encouraging members to keep coming up with ideas that are sparked by others, she promotes creativity.

During the round robin, team leader Madison interjects, "I don't agree with that idea. Seems to me it would cause more problems than it solves." Shawna reminds Madison, "The purpose of this part of the exercise is only to brainstorm as many ideas as possible, not to evaluate them. That will come later."

Third, she reviews the entire list of ideas, which number over 30. As she reads each one aloud, she asks, "Does anyone have any questions about what is meant by this idea?" When questions are raised, she asks the person who contributed the idea to explain it in more detail. She then adds a few more words to that item on the flipchart to capture this fuller understanding. Occasionally, two or three ideas seem quite similar, so she combines them into one, always ensuring that the team agrees that the ideas can be merged without losing some significant distinction between them. By having the group clarify each idea listed, Shawna ensures that all team members have a common understanding of the pool of ideas they now have to work with. The final list contains 16 clearly understood, distinct ideas about how the issue might be resolved. She numbers them "1" through "16" on the left.

Fourth, she asks the members of her team to each privately select his or her favorite five ideas. (The rule of thumb is one-third of the total number of ideas. If the list contains 10 ideas, ask for the favorite three. If the list has 23 ideas, ask for the favorite eight.) Shawna emphasizes, "Please use care in selecting your favorite five. We'll be focusing on the ideas that emerge as the most likely options, and our solution will be built on those that emerge as the team's favorites. So, it's important to be thoughtful in your selections." She asks the team members to make their selections individually, to jot down the item numbers (from 1 to 16) of their favorites, and to not change them even if it turns out that few other people agree.

After allowing time for all to make their selections, she says, "Now I'll read down the list from top to bottom. If the idea is one of your favorite five, raise your hand." As she reads each idea, she writes beside it the number of votes it received. Next she says, "OK, now let's focus on each idea, starting with the ones that received the most votes." By having the team rank the items that have been generated, reported, and clarified, she ensures that the most promising ideas are selected for closer analysis. Voting and ranking also ensures that all members have equal influence in the final selection.

Step 6. Test Options Against Interests and Modify as Necessary

These are the four ideas that got the most votes from Shawna's team:

- Storytellers and analysts need to communicate about the conflict that's being described in the story before it's fully developed, to be sure the story is amenable to analysis (12 votes).
- When one of us disapproves of what another team member is doing, we should go directly to that person and discuss it, and not talk to others about it (11 votes).
- The project team's quality checker needs to review and OK the story before the analyst begins to analyze it (9 votes).
- All specialists need to receive training from David about Mediationworks' quality criteria before production resumes tomorrow, so everyone completely understands the criteria (9 votes).

Shawna says, "In a moment, we'll begin examining each idea that you've come up with, starting with the ones that received the most votes. They are the ones that you as a team think are most likely to help us work together cooperatively to meet our customer's requirements. But first, I'd like for each of you to review your page of interests posted on the wall. Would any of you like to add to or change any of them? Can you honestly say that, if we come up with a plan that does not harm any of those interests, then you can fully support it?"

Storytelling manager Abby says, "Yes, come to think of it, I would like to add an item to my sheet. Looking at the idea that received the most votes makes me aware that I need for my storytellers' creativity to not be diminished by having to submit their stories to analysts for approval."

Wanting to encourage team members to think carefully, Shawna replies, "Good insight, Abby. Let's add some wording to your list of interests." She and Abby discuss how to phrase this new interest. They settle on "To ensure optimum conditions for storytellers' creativity."

Some other members also suggest additions and changes to their lists of interests that are at stake as the team resolves the focal issue. Shawna helps them reword their interests and jots the new wording on the flipchart sheets around the room.

Now Shawna is comfortable that everyone's interests are clarified. She reads the top-ranked idea aloud, then asks, "If we were to include this idea in our action plan, would anyone's interests be negatively affected?"

Predictably, Abby raises a concern about the impact of the top-ranked idea on her storytellers' creative freedom. Shawna asks, "OK, Abby, how might that proposed idea be modified so that storytellers and analysts could communicate early in the process without stifling the storytellers' creativity?" Abby proposes that storytellers first write a one-page overview of the story before the analyst is involved. Together, Shawna and Abby tweak the phrasing of the idea until Abby is comfortable with it.

Shawna continues this process of testing each optional idea against the interests of all team members and modifying it as necessary to ensure that their interests are not harmed. She discontinues the process when they've exhausted the entire list of ideas. She would also stop if they run out of time. (If the mediator discontinues the testing and modifying because of time, he or she should reserve the last half hour or so to complete the mediation.) Depending on the complexity of the team's issue, the number of members, the extent of adversarial climate, and other factors, one to two hours is often sufficient to develop a pool of acceptable ideas that comprise the raw material for an action plan. Under other conditions, it could take one or two days or more to complete. The mediator must always finalize the action plan; a list of acceptable ideas is not enough.

> **Action plan** A set of specific instructions for who is to do what, by when, for how long, with whose support, in what ways, etc. An action plan is *verifiable*. That is, others will be able to determine whether or not individuals have performed their particular tasks as specified in the action plan.

Step 7. Finalize an Action Plan

Returning to the top-ranked idea, which all team members have now explicitly accepted, Shawna asks, "OK, how are we going to accomplish this? Who needs to do what? For how long? By what deadline? With what support from who else? Let's get specific." She leads the group through a discussion of deciding answers to these questions and writes their decisions on a fresh sheet of flipchart paper under the heading "Action Plan."

One element of the action plan is "Storyteller Manager Abby, Analysis Manager Bob, and Team Leaders Madison, Melissa, and Sarah will meet on Friday at 11:00 in Bob's office to develop a schedule for meetings between storytellers and analysts to coordinate the development of stories. Quality Manager David will also be there to review the quality criteria given to us by Mediationworks Press. They will also plan how to enlist the support of all storytellers and analysts for these meetings. Abby will report the resulting plan to Shawna on Monday morning at 9:00."

And so on ... and on ... and on .... Action plans may be— no, they *should* be—very detailed and specific. The action plan is a contract between the team that specifies each individual's responsibilities and each of the members responsible for any of the actions. Any ambiguity should be eliminated by foresight—at least, as much as the players can see in advance. Foresight, unlike hindsight, isn't 20-20. Still, it's easier to solve problems before they happen than after they happen.

Step 8. Ask for Commitment

One step remains to complete Shawna's mediation of her team's conflict. All members need to sincerely confirm that they support the action plan and are committed to implementing it.

Sometimes it's sufficient to simply ask the whole team if everyone buys in, assuming that anyone with reservations will voice them. But it's risky to interpret silence as consent. Shawna wants to ensure that the team's action plan is a collective *consensus* decision—that is, every individual consents to the plan. So, she goes around the room, inviting each individual to express any misgivings about the plan and his or her part in it. Before she asks, she assures them all that she's open to hearing their concerns: "If any of you walk out of this meeting without being fully committed to implementing our action plan, it's at risk of failing. So, it's very important that you voice your concerns now while we have a chance to address them. Also, remember that I'll be holding each of you individually accountable for doing your part of the action plan."

Don't Back Out of the Action   CAUTION!

What if the team blames you, the manager or team leader, for being at fault and contributing to the conflict? You have two options:
- If you are confident that you can openly and non-defensively deal with their criticism, you may still be able to act as the mediator.
- If not, you may consider asking a neutral third party, such as a human resources consultant in your company or a professional facilitator, to act as the mediator. You would then be one of the participants in the team mediation.

You should definitely *not* disengage yourself from the conflict resolution process.

Where's the Conflict?

As you've read about the team conflict at GCSC and observed how Shawna mediated it, you might be wondering, "Where's the conflict? Where's the anger? Where's the bad behavior acknowledged and dealt with?"

Recall that folks at GCSC used walk-aways and power plays as their strategies for handling the situation surrounding them. They sniped, they criticized, they avoided, they ganged up. It was those behaviors that Shawna recognized as conflict. And it was those behaviors that caused the business problem. But notice that Shawna did not explicitly focus on those behaviors during the team mediation. Why not?

Shawna understands that there are three kinds of issues— "matters of concern to the parties"—in every conflict, large or small, interpersonal or international:

- substantive
- emotional
- pseudo-substantive

It's important to identify the issues so that you can deal appropriately with each.

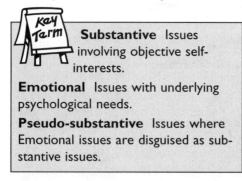

Substantive Issues involving objective self-interests.

Emotional Issues with underlying psychological needs.

Pseudo-substantive Issues where Emotional issues are disguised as substantive issues.

Abby was concerned about optimizing the creativity of her storytellers. Madison was concerned about getting information in a timely manner. These concerns appear quite objective, so they must be substantive issues, right?

But concerns about one's objective self-interests don't cause conflict all by themselves. We know from the situation with Susan and Sean in Chapter 1 that simple disagreement about a substantive issue (in their case, which approach would work best to solve a difficult technical problem) is not the same as conflict.

Emotional issues are present in every situation that fits our definition of conflict—remember the part of that definition that has to do with anger and fault-finding? Emotional issues arise from underlying psychological needs that disputants perceive to be at risk (their frame around the facts), namely:

- **Power**, our need to have influence upon others and for the social status deriving from power differences
- **Approval**, our need for affection, to be liked by others
- **Inclusion,** our need to be accepted as a member of social groups, such as teams at work
- **Justice**, our need to be treated fairly, equally, and equitably
- **Identity**, our needs for autonomy, self-esteem, and affirmation of our personal values

These are universal human needs. True, we may consider them ignoble and we may wish to not have them. Our pop culture heroes seem to be above them. But alas, they are part of our human nature.

In the course of encountering differences in self-interests with others, of framing the situation as having win-lose or lose-lose outcomes, and of behaving competitively because of that frame, something very interesting happens. We generate *pseudo-substantive* issues. That is, we create more matters of concern and proceed to do battle as if they were real, objective underlying interests. In fact, when we are in conflict, we are rarely more than dimly aware of this deception of ourselves and others. We sincerely believe that these issues matter to us, when in fact they don't. We regard them as substantive. We declare our positions on issues that we believe are important to us and we engage in power and rights contests to get our way. We wage war to acquire, preserve, and protect our state of psychological well-being.

The mental gymnastics by which we perform this sleight of mind, this disguising of emotional issues as substantive ones, would take at least a whole book to explain. All Shawna needs to know is that she must treat her team members' self-defined interests *as if* they were real and objective, making no attempt to discern fact from fancy. She simply allows each person the dignity of defining his or her interests while engaging them in a rather mechanical process of solving the business problem. The result? People feel heard, feel respected, and feel validated, which in turn leads to their feeling ownership of and commitment to a solution that they have had a voice in creating.

Shawna focuses on acting as their manager—not as their psychotherapist. That's what she cares about. That's the business issue, the matter of concern to the business.

More Complex Structures

Team mediation is a remarkably flexible tool for resolving conflicts with more complex structures. Fortunately, Shawna was able to use it to resolve a conflict where same-time/same-place communication was possible. But what if she were leader of a virtual team of individuals spread across many time zones?

The same core process can be used when same-time/different-place or even different-time/different-place communication is necessary. But asynchronous communication is fraught with risks—risks of withdrawal and disengagement, risks of inadequate recognition of individuals' interests, and risks of false or superficial commitment to action plans, to name only three. But broadband electronic tools that simulate synchronous communication are emerging as we speak. Our planet is shrinking and we're creating tools that can allow us to overcome, to some extent, differences in time and place.

There's another obstacle that can make mediation more difficult, a factor that complicates the structure of conflict. What would Shawn do if her team members represented constituencies that permitted them little authority to negotiate? Team mediation is more tedious when members have to return to their constituents for approval of proposed ideas. Under those structural conditions, team mediation resembles the seemingly interminable attempts at peacemaking that we read about in our newspapers year after endless year in places like the Middle East, Northern Ireland, Eritrea, and dozens of other trouble spots. In fact, that's exactly what it is.

Manager's Checklist for Chapter 6

❑ Team mediation is a tool for resolving conflicts that have more complex structures than those that can be resolved with managerial mediation and self-mediation.

❑ More advanced facilitation skills are required of the team leader-as-mediator than of the manager-as-mediator or the self-as-mediator.

❑ The steps of team mediation may seem very different from the steps of managerial mediation and self-mediation—at first glance. However, the same underlying process of conflict resolution is happening beneath the procedural surface of the steps that outline the three mediation tools.

How to Mediate All the Time to Prevent Conflicts

Team mediation was a bit complicated. Managerial mediation was simpler: "Mediation without a professional mediator."

Self-mediation was simpler still: "Mediation without a third party."

Preventive mediation is the ultimate in simplicity: "Mediation without an event."

Now, before you professional mediators throw down this book in disgust, give me a moment to defend my heresy against the gospel according to Them. Yes, They ordinarily define mediation as a function that is necessarily performed by a *third* party. And yes, I bent Their definition to near-breaking by describing mediation as a function that a disputant can perform while also negotiating in service of his or her own interests—hence the term, "self-mediation." They had a hard enough time swallowing that strange pill.

But I can see the mutiny taking shape. I can imagine what They might be saying: "Mediation without even a particular occasion for dialogue? That's like hamburger without the beef or water without the wet! Get thee from the Church of Mediation, heretic!"

A Paradigm Shift

Quell the riot. Stay with me a few minutes, a few pages. Join me for a paradigm shift.

Recall my suggestion at the end of Chapter 1 that mediation can be simplified to a "self-help" level of complexity so that all of us can apply its powerful magic to conflicts whose structures are simple enough that a professional level of skill is not needed to resolve them. Managerial mediation and self-mediation are progressively simpler forms of mediation that may be applied to a progressively wider array of human conflicts. That is, we more often need to sort out a conflict with a colleague than we need to step in as a third party.

But even these two simple self-help mediation tools are drawn from our behavioral toolboxes only after a conflict has become noticeable—after it has emerged from the murky depths of unawareness of what's going on in everyday interactions. None of us is fully mindful of others' feelings, interpretive frames, and values and beliefs that constitute the distorting lens through which they view our actions, motives, and intentions. Nor are we fully mindful of our own. Anyone who claims to be fully conscious of his or her inner psychological processes shows, by that very claim, that he or she is even less conscious than the rest of us—if you think you know yourself completely, you don't even know that you don't know!

So, if managerial mediation and self-mediation are dialogue tools designed to be used only after conflicts have become noticeable enough for us to say, "Houston, we've got a problem," isn't there a tool to prevent conflicts from rising to even that modest level of seriousness? What about the lower 90% of the iceberg?

Off-Line, On-Line

Until now, all mediation has been "off-line" intervention. That is, we stop doing whatever we are doing to do mediation. We recognize that we have a problem that must be solved, a conflict that must be resolved, before we can get back to doing our jobs.

Preventive mediation is an "on-line" intervention. That is, it's a way of conducting ourselves with important others that prevents conflicts from becoming so serious that we must stop doing our work to have a dialogue to resolve the conflict that's causing the business problem.

> **Key Term**
>
> **Off-line mediation** Mediation that occurs during an interruption of ordinary work activities, in which negotiation of a disputed issue takes place. All kinds of mediation other than preventive mediation are off-line.

What do we need to do to avoid the dangers submerged in that 90% of the iceberg? How can we prevent conflict before it becomes a problem? Must we develop X-ray vision to peer into the murk? Must we undergo years of psychoanalysis to gain deep insight into our psychological inner workings? Thankfully not. But we may need to undergo a paradigm shift about how we think about conflict and its resolution.

The history of science is a graveyard of dead paradigms—the heliocentric universe, the flat earth, and bloodletting as a cure for disease, to name only three once-prevalent beliefs that outlived their usefulness. As silly as these ideas may seem to us today, the most intelligent, wise, educated people of earlier times held these beliefs, as did the general public who followed their intellectual leadership.

What's the contemporary paradigm, prevalent today, about conflict and its resolution? What do most people now believe to be true? We've already discussed two widely held assumptions that form part of that paradigm:

- "It's best to avoid people with whom I'm in conflict"—the *distancing* wrong reflex.
- "When I'm forced to interact with someone with whom I'm in conflict, it's necessary to do my best to win the (power or rights) contest"—the *coercion* wrong reflex.

Of course, many people might deny that they hold these beliefs, but let's judge by their behavior. Actions speak louder than words in revealing the underlying paradigm: flight or fight.

Earlier chapters described how these two wrong reflexes are deeply rooted in our human nature. Each one of us is the product of an unbroken string of millions of generations of direct ancestors who successfully used these two behavioral strategies to survive in dangerous situations. We may believe that we're better than our ancestors in this respect, but if we listen closely between the lines as our colleagues explain why they behave in conflict as they do, we may hear the *mea non culpa,* "It's not my fault—natural selection made me do it!"

Thankfully, we can, with modest effort at reframing, recognize that our strategic options are not limited to these two reflexes. We can learn to go above and beyond these natural reactions. Every mediator understands the importance of dialogue and engagement between disputants. Every mediator guides the parties toward a both-gain solution to the contest and steers them away from seeking total victory and defeat of the opponent.

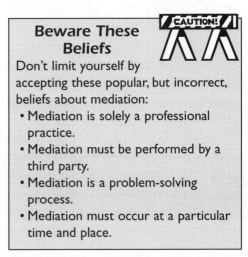

Beware These Beliefs

Don't limit yourself by accepting these popular, but incorrect, beliefs about mediation:

• Mediation is solely a professional practice.
• Mediation must be performed by a third party.
• Mediation is a problem-solving process.
• Mediation must occur at a particular time and place.

But even mediators can be limited by their unquestioned beliefs about conflict. What paradigm still prevails among mediators that is brought into question by preventive mediation? Let's examine some beliefs that are commonly held by mediators, beginning with the least prevalent and progressing toward apostasy:

Belief #1: Mediation is solely a professional practice. If you've stayed with me this far, I trust you are on board with the notion that mediation can be performed effectively by nonprofessionals if the conflict structure is simple enough. In Chapter 4, Eileen showed us how to do managerial mediation.

Beyond the workplace mediation tools proffered in this book, mediation by nonprofessionals is increasingly practiced in

North America and elsewhere in the Western world. Many communities have volunteer mediation programs that provide 30 to 40 hours of basic training, which is enough to enable the volunteers to mediate most landlord-tenant, neighborhood, and small-claims disputes. Another example is the training of resident assistants in many colleges to mediate roommate conflicts.

Belief #2: Mediation must be performed by a third party. Unless you gave up before Chapter 5, you're also on board with the notion that we can do it ourselves. Jay showed us how to do self-mediation.

Belief #3: Mediation is a problem-solving process. Our discussion toward the close of Chapter 6 explained how Shawna adroitly juggled the three kinds of issues (substantive, emotional, pseudo-substantive), successfully resolving a conflict by solving a problem. She understood that problem-solving was just a means to the end of conflict-resolving.

The United States Postal Service has widely adopted a process called "transformative mediation," based on the book *The Promise of Mediation,* by Robert A. Baruch Bush and Joseph P. Folger (Jossey-Bass, 1994). Transformative mediators de-emphasize problem-solving, focusing instead on empowerment of the parties and supporting their recognition of each other. They reverse Shawna's approach: they solve a problem (sometimes) by resolving a conflict. I insert "sometimes" because transformative mediation often does not produce a practical, actionable solution to the very real organizational problem that attracted management's attention to the conflict. Despite my quibbles with their approach, I credit Bush and Folger for challenging the widely held assumption among mediators that mediation in the workplace is, at its core, a problem-solving process and for placing the emphasis on building relationships rather than settling disputes.

Belief #4: Mediation must occur at a particular time and place. Now we're entering the new frontier. Few professionals are with us now, as we boldly go where no mediator has gone before. Let us venture forth.

A Case: Patients-R-Us Hospital

Two years ago the board of directors of Gant General, a 250-bed hospital in Denver, decided to change its name to Patients-R-Us, hoping to produce a correspondingly progressive change in the hospital's image in its surrounding community. Unfortunately, it didn't work. The new Patients-R-Us is still regarded as an undesirable place to go for health care. And its employees know why—the organizational culture stinks. Distrust, hostility, silly turf battles, and petty rivalry are the norm. Staff turnover is high. The place is rife with tension. It could be a case study about conflict.

"Aha!" exclaimed Jacob, the director of staff development, a few months ago. "That's it! I'll use case studies based on typical scenarios here at Patients-R-Us to train our employees to manage conflict better." So Jacob entered "case writing companies" in his favorite Internet search engine and up popped General Case Study Company—our friends from Chapter 6. (By the way, the quality problems that plagued GCSC have been resolved, thanks to Shawna's skillful use of team mediation.) Correspondence with GCSC led to a contract to produce mini-cases that Jacob will use in staff education programs to help Patients-R-Us's employees learn preventive mediation.

Each mini-case stars Nan, the newly hired director of pediatric nursing. Nan reports to Angie, the chief nurse executive of the hospital. Thirty nurses report to Nan through three shift managers. Each mini-case contains the standard three sections (story, analysis, and proposal). The analysis section introduces one distinct concept to help employees think diagnostically about workplace conflict. The proposal section applies that concept in a recommendation for how Nan should use preventive mediation to handle the situation described in the story.

Jacob expects that once employees have completed the series of mini-case studies in guided classroom activities, they will be able to use preventive mediation on the job at Patients-R-Us, accomplishing its transformation from dysfunctional Gant General to a healthier health care institution. Let's take a look at the mini-cases that Jacob bought from GCSC.

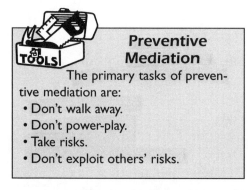

Preventive Mediation

The primary tasks of preventive mediation are:

• Don't walk away.
• Don't power-play.
• Take risks.
• Don't exploit others' risks.

Mini-Case 1

Title: Preventive Mediation
Primary Task #1: Don't walk away
Story: Nan and Dr. Nick Connor, an anesthesiologist, are like oil and water. Both have a clear but unspoken sense that they just don't like each other, although the reasons aren't entirely clear. Maybe they remind each other of difficult people they've known in the past. Whatever the reason, they would just as soon not have anything to do with each other. But, work at Patients-R-Us being what it is, that's not possible. As the most experienced and senior anesthesiologist in the hospital, Nick is called in when patients in Nan's department require serious surgery. Nick's services are needed in pediatric surgery for emergency cases several times each month and it's Nan's responsibility to call him when these surgeries are scheduled. So, they have fairly frequent interactions. When calls to him are necessary, Nan is not rude, but she's not particularly friendly, either. She gets right to the point with no small talk, schedules the surgery, mutters "thanks," and hangs up. When Nan and Nick pass each other in the hall, they both look straight ahead or at the floor, never at each other. On occasion, when Nan calls him regarding an upcoming surgery, Nick says he's already scheduled to assist with surgery in another department. She suspects that Nick prefers not to assist in emergency pediatric surgeries because he doesn't like her, not because he's already scheduled elsewhere. In fact, she has confirmed that his excuse didn't hold water on at least two occasions. When Nick is not available, she must ask an anesthesiologist from another specialty area to assist, which increases the risk of suboptimal patient care.

Analysis: Both Nan and Nick are distancing. That is, they avoid each other whenever possible, as evidenced by Nan's curtness on the phone and their lack of eye contact when passing in the hall. These behaviors are examples of walk-aways, which are the behavioral manifestation of the distancing wrong reflex. Their distancing wouldn't matter except that they have an ongoing interdependent relationship and need to interact effectively. Patient care could be affected by their poor relationship. That risk constitutes the business problem caused by their distancing behavior.

Proposal: Nan should cease distancing and engage more directly with Nick. When she calls him by phone, she could sprinkle the conversation with pleasantries such as "Good afternoon, Dr. Connor, how are you today?" or "I heard you won the all-staff golf tournament last Sunday—congratulations!" or "I really appreciate your help with the surgery on Baby Moore last week. I understand that the timing wasn't convenient for you, and we really needed your expertise." Nan also could engage Nick when they pass in the hall. She could look him in the eye and say with a smile, "Good morning, Dr. Connor," or a similar friendly greeting. By unilaterally breaking their pattern of mutual distancing, Nan would break the cycle of subtle retaliation that causes their conflict to persist and threatens the quality of patient care.

Discussion of the Mini-Case

This case illustrates distancing, its potential consequences, and a proposed action for Nan to reduce it. The case also introduces another useful concept—the "retaliatory cycle" (Figure 7-1).

The retaliatory cycle is the anatomy of interpersonal conflict. When we place a specimen of human conflict under the X-ray machine to see through the superficial soft tissue of appearances, we discern the skeleton. The three classical realms of psychology become visible: 1) cognition, the thinking process, 2) emotion, the feeling process, and 3) behavior, the doing process. That's all there is to us, psychologically.

Only the behavioral part is visible to others. Only verbal and nonverbal behaviors are observable. You can't see my thoughts and feelings. You can only infer them indirectly by interpreting

Key Term **Retaliatory cycle** A *triggering event* leads to one's *perception* that his or her interests are threatened (cognition, or thinking), which leads to *anger* (emotion, or feeling), which leads to *acting out* by means of walkaways or power plays (behavior, or doing), which serves as a *triggering event* leading to the other's perception that his or her interests are threatened ... and so on.

my observable behavior. You *see* my scowl and you *infer* that *I feel* angry. You *hear* my disagreeing statement and you *infer* that *I think* you are incompetent. (Does "framing" come to mind here? If so, you get a gold star!)

Nan and Nick are locked in a retaliatory

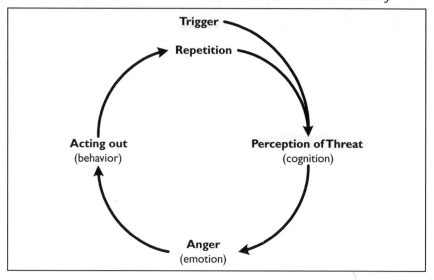

Figure 7-1. The retaliatory cycle

cycle, although it's one of low intensity. Nan is reacting to Nick's reactions to Nan's earlier reactions to Nick's still earlier reactions ... and so on. Their distancing behavior is subtle but discernable—their walk-aways (e.g., avoidance of eye contact) act out their feelings (e.g., dislike, resentment) toward each other. So, their conflict is not one that calls for off-line mediation, even that simplest kind we call self-mediation. But their conflict is incurring cost—risk of inferior patient care.

By her unilateral choice to not react to Nick's walk-aways with walk-aways of her own, Nan breaks the retaliatory cycle.

Recall our discussion in Chapters 4 and 5 of how conciliatory gestures are used in managerial mediation and self-mediation. Nan's shift to non-threatening, friendly, even vulnerable behavior may elicit corresponding behavior from Nick—if not today, then perhaps tomorrow, or the next day, or the next. His reciprocating gesture would be low-risk: simply replying "hello" to Nan in the hallway or smiling in response to her smile exposes him to little risk.

So, by simply opting not to continue her part of the pattern of distancing, Nan is intervening on-line—that is, while ordinary workplace activities are going on—to prevent the continuation of this seemingly minor conflict with Nick. She's practicing "preventive mediation."

Mini-Case 2

Title: Preventive Mediation Primary Task #2: Don't power-play
Story: Lindsay, one of the most technically skilled nurses in the pediatric nursing department, calls Nan's secretary, Lisa, to arrange a meeting for tomorrow afternoon. Nan has asked her staff to state the purpose of requested meetings so she can prepare and so she can triage the many demands on her busy schedule. But when Lisa asked Lindsay to state the purpose of the meeting, Lindsay replied, "I'll tell her when I get there." Nan felt annoyed that Lindsay didn't disclose the purpose of the requested meeting. "If I don't know how important the meeting is, how am I supposed to know whether it's something I can reschedule if a more critical issue comes up?" she mutters to herself rhetorically.

It's now time for their meeting and Lindsay is a few minutes late, which annoys Nan even more. "Not only does Lindsay not respect my request to give the purpose of the meeting, she doesn't even respect my time by being prompt!"

When Lindsay finally arrives, she offers no apology for her tardiness, but immediately announces her reason for the meeting. "There's a problem with Daniel, that new nurse you hired," Lindsay begins. "He's right out of school and doesn't have the experience to work with preemies. But he acts like he's at the same level as the rest of us. Besides, as a male, he just can't give the same quality of care as a female nurse. I want you to make sure he's not assigned to work with preemies or very sick kids. I don't want to work in a peds department where care of sick babies is not the top priority," she concludes.

Nan is still fuming about Lindsay's discourtesy as she listens to what seems to her an inappropriate and rather insubordinate demand. And she hears Lindsay's final remark as a threat that she'll quit if Nan doesn't do as she wants. "What an impudent pup!" she thinks to herself.

Analysis: Lindsay's demand regarding Daniel's assignments and her implied threat of quitting are power plays. Nan is strongly tempted to respond with a higher card in the same suit. Indeed, as Lindsay's hierarchical superior, she has the authority to disregard her pushy demands. She could also scold Lindsay for failing to follow standard procedures in setting up their meeting. If Nan did so, she would be using a power play (coercion) to act out her angry feelings, retaliating against Lindsay. But trumping Lindsay's power play with a more powerful power play would not help solve the administrative issue of Daniel's assignments. Suppose for a moment that Lindsay's assessment of his suitability as a nurse with the most vulnerable babies is correct or even contains just a kernel of truth. If Nan disregards that information brought to her attention, babies could be at risk of receiving substandard care.

Proposal: Nan should not succumb to the temptation of using a power play (overriding Lindsay by discounting her complaint about Daniel) to act out her anger about how Lindsay set up their meeting. Instead, she should consider Lindsay's input about Daniel's competencies along with perhaps more objective sources of information in handling that administrative matter. Furthermore, she should respond assertively, not aggressively, to Lindsay. (Recall our distinction between *assertive* and *aggressive* in Chapter 5.) She could say, "Lindsay, I appreciate your bringing your concerns about Daniel to my attention. I'll consider your opinions and wishes. I would also like to remind you to give Lisa the purpose of meetings when you request them in the future. I need your cooperation on this. May I have it, please?"

Discussion of the Mini-Case

This case illustrates coercion and its potential consequences and it proposes that Nan respond non-coercively despite her impulse to use power plays. The case also reminds us of the how to behave assertively, not aggressively, in response to power plays.

So, by opting not to power-play when the natural urge to retaliate is strong, Nan is mediating on-line. She's practicing preventive mediation.

Mini-Case 3

Title: Preventive Mediation Primary Task #3: Take risks
Story: Delores is a very good nurse who has exceptional medical knowledge and clinical skills. She has become a certified lactation consultant on her own time and at her own expense. Clearly, she is dedicated to her profession and performs above standards.

But Delores' coworkers avoid her like the plague. She is hypercritical of other nurses, openly pointing out even the slightest errors they make. And it seems she never gets up on the right side of the bed—her coworkers call her "BM," which, in this case, stands for "Bad Mood." She's strictly business all the time, making no effort to be sociable and friendly with others. With patients, she is sensitive and attentive, if not warm. She receives very good evaluations from new moms for her expert assistance in getting them started with breast-feeding.

Delores treats Nan the same as she does her coworkers, freely criticizing her for the many mistakes she thinks Nan is making in her new position as Director of Pediatric Nursing. When the two met recently about scheduling Delores' lactation consults, Delores recited a list of shortcomings in Nan's performance. Nan considers herself a good nurse and a good, if new, manager. Still, Delores' criticisms, unleavened by even a scintilla of praise, are hard for her to listen to.

Analysis: It's understandable that Nan perceives Delores' criticisms as threats to her self-interests. Foremost among her interests during this encounter is the need to preserve her self-esteem, which is under attack. This arouses an emotional issue within Nan (recall our discussion of the three kinds of issues in Chapter 5). Unconsciously, she could disguise the emotional issue as a pseudo-substantive one, such as criticizing Delores in return for lacking a good team attitude. Feeling vulnerable under the assault of her fault-finding, Nan finds it hard to be complimentary of Delores, despite her exceptional nursing skills.

Proposal: Nan should override her natural defensive impulse to retaliate, instead taking the risk of offering conciliatory gestures to Delores. She could say, "Delores, you're a keen observer. This new position is indeed very challenging and I'm sometimes unsure how well I'm doing. It's helpful to hear your suggestions." She could also compliment Delores, saying, "Your expertise as a lactation consultant is a real asset to this department. I really appreciate the work you've done to contribute that competency to our range of services."

Nan should stifle every impulse to react with counter-criticism. Instead, she should think of herself as a "spear-catcher" who willingly absorbs the blows of her "adversary," safe in the knowledge that she will not be damaged by Delores' verbal spears. Indeed, she may invite more: "Delores, what other suggestions do you have for me? What other mistakes do you think I've made so far?" By non-defensively receiving these verbal barbs, Nan frames them as opportunities to allow Delores to discharge her own pent-up feelings. Nan understands that Delores' penchant for hypercriticism is an outward expression of her inner vulnerability, fear, and anger, which have unknown but psychologically primitive origins far outside their immediate workplace. (Indeed, this is a safe assumption in every situation where people are aggressively critical of others—they're unconsciously attempting to shield their own vulnerabilities by using the misapplied principle that "the best defense is a good offense." This may be a useful tactic for winning wars and football games, but not for winning voluntary cooperation from others.) So, by taking the risk of serving as a spear-catcher, Nan is likely to eventually enlist Delores' support, respect, and appreciation.

Discussion of the Mini-Case

Recall the childhood taunt, "Sticks and stones may break my bones but words will never hurt me"? It's simply the child's perceptual reframe of other children's verbal attacks. The new frame protects the child from gratuitous criticism from peers.

On a grander scale, Mohandas Gandhi elevated nonviolence to an art form. His strategy of nonviolence succeeded where a conventional military power contest offered no hope of success in India's independence movement from Britain in the 1940s. He brilliantly reframed his country's struggle.

In a similar fashion, but on a smaller scale, Nan reframes her struggle to enlist Delores' support as a constructive team player in the pediatric nursing department. Clearly, no amount of coercive power play would succeed in changing Delores' workplace behavior. There is no guarantee that "interpersonal nonviolence" will succeed either, but it's a far more powerful strategy than the reflexive power contest that less wise managers than Nan might employ in their misguided attempts to win unwinnable conflicts. There is much to gain and nothing to lose but a temporarily bruised ego. Paradoxically, taking risks is more powerful than using power plays. By taking the risk of extending conciliatory gestures in response to Delores' aggressiveness, Nan is practicing preventive mediation.

Mini-Case 4

Title: Preventive Mediation Primary Task #4: Don't exploit others' risks

Story: Andrew, the director of nursing for the outpatient department, got married on short notice and moved from Denver to Salt Lake City, where his spouse lives. Andrew's sudden departure left chief nurse executive Angie scrambling to find a suitable replacement. While a search is under way, Angie asked

Nan and Gary, who is Nan's counterpart in the emergency department, to consider covering Andrew's duties until a full-time replacement could be found. Neither Nan nor Gary wants to take on this extra responsibility and they've both made their wishes known to Angie. However, Angie needs temporary coverage of outpatient nursing and she calls the two into her office to discuss the situation and decide who is going to do the job. (Angie could simply assign Nan or Gary to take over for Andrew, but she's learned by observing Nan's excellent conflict resolution skills that it would be better if the replacement accepted the new duties voluntarily.)

Angie begins the meeting by describing the problem and her reasons for needing either Gary or Nan to cover Andrew's duties for a month or so until she finds his replacement.

Gary explains, "Look, unlike most peds patients, emergency patients are emergencies. They're unscheduled. So I can't plan my nurses' time to free me up to cover the outpatient department. Nan could do that. Besides, over half of outpatients are kids anyway, so it would be a natural fit for Nan."

Nan explains, "Look, I've been on the job here at Patients-R-Us for only a couple of months. I'm still getting my feet on the ground. Besides, I've inherited some personnel problems that I've got to resolve before I can turn my attention elsewhere. This is not the time for me to take on another department. Gary has the experience to handle it."

This game of hot potato continues for several minutes, Gary and Nan both trying to pass the unwanted duties to the other before they get burned by having to take over outpatient nursing. After a while, Gary says, "Well, it's true that a lot of emergency admissions are not actual emergencies. Lots of people with noncritical problems come to the ER because they don't know where else to go. Many of them could be handled in the outpatient clinic."

Analysis: Gary's last comment is a conciliatory gesture. Nan could exploit his act of voluntary vulnerability by agreeing that his statement is correct and therefore he should take over the outpatient department. But if she did so, Gary would likely experience that reaction as punishment for trying to be cooperative. If Nan exploited Gary's risk, it might enable her to win this particular battle, but would not help build an ongoing collaborative relationship with him.

Proposal: Nan should respond cooperatively to Gary, matching his conciliatory gesture with one of her own. She could say, "Gary, I appreciate you being open-minded about this. It's also true that many of the emergency admissions that are not true emergencies are also kids. If you could take primary responsibility for outpatient, I could assign a peds nurse to emergency to help triage admissions so non-emergency kids could be brought directly to my department. Would that help?"

Discussion of the Mini-Case

By responding to Gary's risk-taking comment with a reciprocal conciliatory gesture, Nan breaks the retaliatory cycle and prompts a breakthrough—the mutual attitude shift we discussed in Chapter 4. Previously adversaries, Gary and Nan are now planning how to cooperatively cover the duties left vacated by the departing Andrew. Their previous attitudes of "me against you" have become "us against the problem." Angie must be pleased as she listens to their exchange. She's probably taking mental notes about how valuable these two department directors are to the hospital! By not exploiting the risk that Gary took in exploring a both-gain solution, rather than win-lose, Nan is practicing preventive mediation.

Thinking Tools

The four primary tasks of preventive mediation are hardly rocket science. They are just common sense. You don't need a college degree to understand them. But as easy as they are to understand, they may be equally difficult to perform.

Jacob recognizes that employees at Patients-R-Us may need some "thinking tools" to help them implement the simple behavioral prescriptions to not walk away, to not power-play, to take risks, and to not exploit others' risks. GCSC has written two mini-cases to help employees learn two key thinking tools.

Mini-Case 5

Title: Preventive Mediation Thinking Tool #1: Feelings as data
Story: Kyle is the third-shift ward clerk on the pediatric floor. In his late 40s, he's one of the old-timers who worked at Gant General Hospital for a long time before its recent breach rebirth as Patients-R-Us. Indeed, if his coworkers' comments are correct, Kyle personifies the culture of the old Gant General. Since she took the position of director of pediatric nursing a couple of months ago, Nan has come to understand why they call him "Kyle Gant." Kyle barks at nurses who dare to ask him to do anything that's not strictly within his job description. His standard retort is "That's not my job, so it must be yours." He is usually irritable and unfriendly, so floor nurses avoid him as much as possible. Kyle's behavior makes it even more difficult to retain good nurses to work third shift, which is a challenging staffing problem under the best of circumstances.

> **Key Term**
>
> **Thinking tools** Intentional reframes of one's perceptions, assumptions, and attributions that enable us to act strategically during conflict, rather than acting reflexively and defensively. Two especially effective thinking tools in preventive mediation are:
> #1: Feelings as data
> #2: Owning my own experience

Last week, Kristie, one of the best nurses on third shift, came to Nan in tears. "I can't take it any longer," Kristie cried. "It's either Kyle or me. Give me another shift or I'm outta here." Kristie's complaint was the final nudge Nan needed to schedule a performance review with Kyle, which she set for the next morning at 7:00, at the end of his shift.

Right on time, Kyle strode brusquely into her office and sat down without saying a word. His body language screamed, "Just *dare* to try to fire me!" Nan began by carefully and objectively outlining her concerns about the atmosphere on third shift. But after only a couple of minutes, Kyle abruptly interrupted her, almost shouting, "You don't have a clue what's going on at night on my ward! You might think you're little miss executive here at the 'new' hospital, but let me tell you, you're gonna get eaten alive if you don't watch out!"

Nan felt almost physically knocked back, startled by the vehemence in Kyle's voice. A storm of feelings welled up inside her—contempt for Kyle and fear that her future at Patients-R-Us may not turn out as rosy as she'd assumed. Memories of the supervisor she had on her first job out of nursing school popped into her mind, a man whom she detested and who fired her from that first job. She suddenly and vividly recalled her painful disillusionment about the nursing profession, when she nearly decided to quit nursing altogether. Barely maintaining her composure, Nan was on the verge of stopping this meeting and immediately going the personnel office to begin termination action against Kyle. At the same time, she was aware that firing a combative long-term employee is fraught with difficulties.

Analysis: Strong emotions are evident in this story: Kyle's anger, Nan's contempt and fear. Also very strong is her impulse to act out her feelings by halting the meeting with Kyle (distancing) and trying to fire him (coercion). Without doubt, she faces an administrative crisis about staffing the third shift: she's got to do something about the loss of good employees due to the behavior of this marginal performer. The organizational issue is how Nan can most effectively manage the strong emotions—Kyle's and her own—and make the right decision about third-shift staffing.

Proposal: Nan should reframe Kyle's hostility, and her own emotional reaction to it, with the "feelings-as-data" thinking tool. Despite feeling victimized, she is not without choices here. Unlike many people, Nan knows that she has a cognitive choice as well as a behavioral choice. In the behavioral realm, she can choose whether to verbally snap back at Kyle and she can choose whether to go to personnel to fire him. But in the cognitive realm, she can also choose how to *think* about his anger, as well as about her own feelings of contempt and fear.

Let's first consider her response to Kyle. Nan can choose to regard his anger simply as objective data, much as she might dispassionately regard the crying of an infant in neonatal intensive care. She would use the baby's crying as a diagnostic clue for what might be causing its distress. Her goal would be to diagnose and solve the infant's medical problem.

Using this thinking tool, she could ask herself, "I wonder what is causing Kyle to be so angry at me?" or "I wonder what may be happening on the ward that makes him irritable and uncooperative?" or "I see that Kyle is unhappy in his job, yet he protects it fiercely. I wonder how he deals with that ambivalence?" Applying the thinking tool, she could ask him exploratory questions, instead of reflexively reacting to him out of her own defensive anger. She may ask, "Kyle, I see that you're very upset with me. Can you help me understand why?" or "I'm puzzled about how you seem to love your job and hate it at the same time. What's that like for you?" or "You seem to be giving me a warning. I'd like to know what you see as the dangers in my new job here." Her goal would be to diagnose and solve the hospital's staff problem.

By regarding Kyle's feelings as objective data, Nan is able to step aside from his aggressive thrusts, avoiding becoming enmeshed in a power contest, which she would surely lose. (Recall our discussion in Chapter 3 about the self-defeating result of "winning" power and rights contests with people whose voluntary cooperation we'll need in the future.) By using this thinking tool, she's able to remain non-adversarial in their dialogue as she explores what may be done to address the administrative problem of Kyle's job performance.

Importantly, she is able to engage non-adversarially *without his cooperation*. That is, she is not dependent on Kyle's changing how he's behaving toward her. She's empowered by using the feelings-as-data thinking tool to be in control of their encounter.

Next, let's consider how Nan can handle her own emotions. Using the thinking tool, she chooses to objectively consider her own feelings of contempt and fear. Noting that vivid memories of her first job as a nurse came to mind, she may ask herself, "I wonder if my reaction to Kyle is influenced by my experience with my first supervisor?" or "I wonder if my fear in this situation is magnified by the trauma I experienced when I was fired from my first job and felt terrified that I'd made the wrong career choice?"

> ## Thinking Tool: Feelings as Data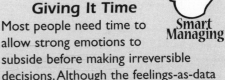
> When emotions arise during conflict, choose to frame them as factual, objective information and to treat them as you would treat other factual data. What do they reveal about what's happening in the other person and what's happening in you.

Discussion of the Mini-Case

The encounter between Nan and Kyle was intensely emotional. The proposal illustrates how Nan can use the feelings-as-data thinking tool when conflict is intense.

But its value is not limited to such volatile situations. Indeed, its greatest value is realized when the tool becomes second nature, when it becomes a habit so ingrained that we're hardly conscious of it. When we routinely and automatically view feelings as data, it sharply diminishes our tendency to react angrily and defensively.

It's like riding a bicycle. It might take you a lot of effort and focus to learn, but once you learn, you don't have to think about it—and you never forget. The new habit enters your "body memory."

> ## Giving It Time
> ### Smart Managing
> Most people need time to allow strong emotions to subside before making irreversible decisions. Although the feelings-as-data thinking tool empowers you to stay engaged in a dialogue in a non-adversarial way, it's unlikely that you can get completely free yourself from the biasing effect of those emotions on your decisions. It's best to wait a while before deciding to take action. Use the passage of time as your ally.

But our old slippers feel good, comfortably familiar. Some readers may be clinging to warm, fuzzy perceptual frames like "You shouldn't make me feel this way" and "You shouldn't be angry at me." Notice how these frames keep us dependent on the other to accept our "should's," our expectations. But we shouldn't "should" on each other! We may not like the fact that others have the feelings they do—or that we ourselves feel as we do. But feelings are just that—facts, whether we like it or not. We can choose how to act and we can choose how to think, but we can't choose how to feel.

Our choice in life is either to rail against cruel fate or to play the hand we're dealt. Which choice yields the better life? Our choice in conflict is either to rail against unwanted feelings or to accept their objective existence. Which choice yields the better resolution?

By using the feelings-as-data thinking tool, Nan is able to 1) respond dispassionately to Kyle's hostility toward her and 2) reflect analytically upon her own strong emotions. This will undoubtedly help her arrive at a more rational and better decision about how to manage Kyle. By framing feelings as data, Nan is practicing preventive mediation.

Mini-Case 6

Title: Preventive Mediation Thinking Tool #2: Owning my own experience

Story:

Scene 1: It's December 15. Everyone is looking forward to the winter holidays. Several pediatric nurses have requested extra days off to spend with their families and Nan has done her best to accommodate their wishes. Upon checking her in-box this morning, Nan finds a memo from chief nurse executive Angie to all nursing staff announcing that, because of an outbreak of influenza, all nurses will be required to work their full schedules. No extra days off will be allowed. Nan receives the memo at the same time as everyone else. She mumbles to herself, "Well, if Angie Napoleon isn't at it again! Overriding my authority like that! We're pediatric nurses, not medical/surgical nurses. Does she think the flu is going to suddenly create more babies! She really annoys me!"

Scene 2: During the weekly staff meeting with her three shift managers, Nan reports summary results of the hospital's satisfaction survey, which is given to every patient at the time of discharge. Over the past three weeks there's been a decline in overall patient satisfaction with nursing service on the second shift. Nan expresses her concern about the decline to Trish, the second-shift manager, and reminds staff of the importance of ensuring that patients have a positive experience with all nursing staff. Later that day, Trish comes to Nan's office complaining, "Nan, you embarrassed me by making me look bad in the staff meeting this morning. You made me angry."

Analysis: In scene 1, Nan attributes the cause of her annoyance to Angie. Her perceptual frame is that there's a direct causal link between the memo and her negative feelings. In scene 2, Trish attributes the cause of her embarrassment and anger to Nan. Trish's perceptual frame is that there's a direct causal link between the discussion of survey data in the staff meeting and her negative feelings. In neither scene do the protagonists recognize that there's an interpretive process going on, that there may be another way of understanding how and why they're feeling as they do.

Proposal: In scene 1, Nan should reframe her perception of what causes her to be annoyed in response to Angie's memo. She should use the "owning my own experience" thinking tool to take responsibility for her emotional reactions to external events—that is, things that happen outside her skin. She could ask herself, "I seem to get really annoyed when a senior person overrides my authority. I wonder why that's so?" or "I know that other people might experience this situation differently. How might my old mentor, Guthrie, perceive Angie's memo if he were in my moccasins?" or (putting herself in Angie's moccasins) "I wonder what Angie's frame was when she sent that memo?" These reframes place Nan in control of her experience, rather than in the role of a helpless victim who can only react automatically to Angie's action.

In scene 2, Nan should coach Trish to consider alternative interpretations of the discussion of patient satisfaction data in the staff meeting. She could tell her, "I see that you're upset by the way I handled the discussion about patient satisfaction surveys. Maybe I could have done that with more sensitivity. I'm also curious about how you may be interpreting what was said in the meeting. What do you think my intentions were? Did it seem to you that I intended to put you on the spot?"

Discussion of the Mini-Case

Every behavior during social interactions has an *intention* and an *effect*. We say things because we want to affect others in a desired way. But the effect of what we say is often very different from what we intended.

In scene 1, Angie's intention in issuing the memo was to ensure adequate nursing coverage during an expected outbreak of the flu. Its unintended effect was Nan's defensive anger about her authority being overridden. Recalling the "perception of threat" stage of the retaliatory cycle, we understand that Nan made attributions to Angie that probably did not exist, such as disrespect for Nan's authority.

In scene 2, Nan's intention in discussing patient satisfaction was to urge her staff to be more attentive to giving patients a positive experience with their nursing care. Its unintended effect was Trish's defensive anger about looking bad in front of her peers. Understanding the retaliatory cycle, we recognize that Trish made incorrect attributions to Nan, such as unconcern about Trish's social and professional status among the staff.

Nan's and Trish's attributions occurred in the absence of significant conflict. Misunderstandings of intentions are far more likely when there's a conflict that's escalating and the retaliatory cycle is well under way. Any professional mediator will confirm that in every conflict parties' perceptions of their adversaries' intentions are severely distorted. And the distortion is in a predictable direction—toward the negative. Adversaries do not give the benefit of the doubt where intentions are ambiguous—and the others' intentions are *always* ambiguous, since we don't have direct knowledge of their cognitive processes. Adversaries usually perceive hostile intentions where none exist. Incorrect attributions flourish in the toxic soil of conflict.

Using the owning-my-own-experience thinking tool enables us to avoid this perceptual trap in two ways:

1. By understanding (framing) that there's not a direct causal link between your behavioral actions and my emotional reactions, I remain in control of my experience of our relationship. I'm driving the bus that carries my feelings; I'm not a passenger on *your* bus.
2. By understanding (framing) that there's a high risk—especially when I am angry—that I'm attributing intentions to you that don't exist, I'm able to consider the possibility that the effect that I'm experiencing didn't come from *you*. Gee, maybe it came from *me*! Maybe it's my own interpretive process that's causing me to feel as I do!

By using this thinking tool to reframe her interaction with Angie and by coaching Trish to reframe her experience of their interaction, Nan is practicing preventive mediation.

Completing the Paradigm Shift

This chapter may have challenged some old familiar ways of thinking that you've long held dear. The primary tasks of preventive mediation can be difficult for us. It's comforting to our sore and battered egos to behave in the same old ways. It's a relief to walk away. It gives us (the illusion of) dignity to power-play. It's safer to not take risks. It feels like victory to exploit others' risks.

And it's a reassuring illusion that we can wish feelings—our own and those of others—to be different or gone. And it's a balm of soothing innocence to believe that others are responsible for the way I feel.

But in the new paradigm, we clearly understand that these are false hopes and false beliefs, just as people of recent centuries came to clearly understand that the sun is not the center of the universe, that the earth is not flat, and that bloodletting does not cure disease.

Few of us will join the ranks of Mohandas Gandhi, Nelson Mandela, and Martin Luther King, Jr., who led great nonviolent social movements. But every one of us can use some of their

> ### Outside the Box
> **Smart Managing** There's a bonus in going outside the traditional paradigm to practice preventive mediation: you become better at "thinking outside the box." Not only do you become better at dealing with conflicts and avoiding problems, but you also develop your ability to step outside of conventional paths and think more creatively.

principles in the form of preventive mediation in our workplaces to resolve conflicts on-line, before they escalate enough to emerge from the murk and become noticeable disputes. Perhaps you also have other important relationships, outside of work, where the old paradigm has not served you well— your family, your spouse, your children. Maybe it's time to lead a peaceful revolution in your own little corner of the world?

Manager's Checklist for Chapter 7

❑ Preventive mediation is a tool for resolving conflicts before they become problems.

❑ Because of the prevailing paradigm of widely held beliefs about conflict and how it can be managed, preventive mediation may seem counter-intuitive and contrarian.

❑ The four primary tasks that constitute preventive mediation are simple to understand but it can be challenging to do them. This chapter offers two thinking tools to help you perform those tasks.

Strategic Management of Organizational Conflict

S o far we've learned four specific mediation tools: managerial mediation, self-mediation, team mediation, and preventive mediation. And, we've learned *when* to use them by understanding conflict structure. Gold star readers may even have internalized a "contingency model" of mediation, enabling you to modify these tools to fit a particular conflict by considering its structure.

"Are we there yet?" you ask from the back seat. "Is that all I need to manage conflict at work?"

"Nope, we're one-third of the way to our destination," your patient chauffeur replies.

"Only a third!" you exclaim in surprise. "But this is the last chapter of the book. Where's the other two-thirds?"

Let's look another case study to see how organizational conflict can strategically managed. Keep in mind that this is not just good for everyone's peace of mind. Doing this has many positive business consequences.

Planning for Contingencies

Smart Managing   The mediation tools in this book are designed for commonplace but specific conflict structures. By thinking about how each tool fits each structure, you can develop a "contingency model" of workplace mediation. That means you can modify a tool that almost—but not quite—fits the conflict you hope to resolve by carefully comparing the structure of your conflict with the structure of the kind of conflict for which the tool is designed with a few well-considered tweaks.

A Case: Mediation Training Institute International, Inc.

Mediation Training Institute International (MTI) is an employee-owned global company with $8 billion annual sales, a figure that has risen sharply each year since The Great Paradigm Shift of 2001. In that year, a critical mass of the world's population grasped the fact that faithful readers of this book know—that everyday conflicts can be prevented, managed, and resolved more successfully by reconciling interests than by contesting rights and power. Its significance has been likened to the paradigm shift of the 1490s when people finally grasped the fact that the earth is a sphere. As a result of this paradigm shift, most of the planet's six billion cohabitants now unquestioningly accept that conflict is a resolvable, manageable, and preventable process—not an inevitability that must simply be tolerated. They know as certainly as the earth is round that, although differences are inevitable, conflict is not. So countless attorneys have had to find other means of livelihood. Lawyer jokes have mostly disappeared from lack of grist. The few saber-rattling politicians who remain in office are viewed as curious anachronisms and are rarely re-elected. Mediation training has become an explosive growth industry.

MTI's mission is "To train everyone everywhere to use mediation everyday." About a thousand of the company's 20,000 employees work at MTI's headquarters in Arlington, Virginia, across the Potomac from Washington, D.C. The other 19,000 work in MTI's field offices, which are located in every national capital and major city in the world. In addition to its employee-owners, MTI has trained and certified over two million independent Certified Mediation Trainers (CMTs) worldwide who train and coach people in every sector of every society to use mediation tools. MTI is organized into divisions that provide services in each sector—the largest divisions of the company are Corporate, Judicial, School, Environmental, Family, and Political. Through its CMTs and its Web-based training programs offered in over 120 languages, MTI has so far trained nearly three billion people to use mediation tools wherever they live and work. Despite its great size, MTI is a remarkably flat organization, owing to its use of cutting-edge Internet and wireless technology.

Seamus is President and CEO of MTI. (Yes, Seamus is the same young college graduate we glimpsed on the opening page of this book as he wrestled with the decision of which job offer to accept—he opted for the dotcom.) He downloaded a copy of this book from Nile.com, his favorite online bookseller, and is reading it on his e-book. But he's found nothing new in it so far. MTI already has developed popular training programs that enable people to use the mediation tools it describes. "SOS," he mutters to himself. "Same old stuff. Just another author rehashing the SOS that other authors have rehashed, over and over. These recovering academics are all the same. When is someone going to come up with something new in mediation?"

Sitting in his office overlooking the National Mall, Seamus gazes at the Capitol dome gleaming under the morning sun, which only reminds him of more SOS. Discouraged, he's about to press the delete key on his e-book when he reaches the final chapter—the one you're reading right now. "Hmmm ... 'strategic management of organizational conflict.' What the hell does that mean?"

Seamus uses his voice-to-text device to send a note to Bruce, MTI's VP for Corporate Services, who is on a flight from Johannesburg to Singapore at the moment. Seamus' note pops up on Bruce's in-flight screen as he's finishing the evening meal of ostrich steak accented by a fine Stellenbosch cabernet.

"What's 'strategic management of organizational conflict?'" the note reads. Bruce immediately replies, "Never heard of it." Seamus ponders, "Maybe this is something new. I'll look into it."

The Three Strategies

Every organization has a strategy for managing conflict ... but few know what it is. Every individual has a strategy for managing conflict ... and we've learned what that is—the wrong reflexes of distancing and coercion that we've inherited from our animal ancestors and that cripple us today.

Whether as individuals or as organizations, we manage conflict. Conflict happens, and we deal with it. We use the tools that are in our toolbox. If we want to insert a screw in a block of wood, and the only tool we have is a hammer, we use the hammer. If our paradigm is "hammers are the right tool for inserting screws," we don't know what we're missing.

Some readers may have discovered in previous pages that they've been missing something. They've discovered a shiny new tool. They've discovered that the essential process of mediation (recall Chapter 3) is a better strategy than are the wrong reflexes for managing differences in ongoing interdependent relationships and for preventing small conflicts from escalating into serious and costly big ones.

That personal discovery is the first step toward strategic management of *interpersonal* conflict. Organizations, too, may discover that their current conflict management strategy is ineffective. The instrument given in Chapter 2 for measuring the financial cost of conflict can spark that awareness.

Using that instrument, Seamus does a quick calculation of the cost of conflict in MTI. He's dismayed that, despite its thousands of employees being expert conflict resolvers, there's still conflict in his company. And that conflict is costing money. How can that be? Like Roy in Chapter 2, Seamus is now paying attention.

Most of MTI's training programs contain reference to the three and only three ways to manage conflict: by power contests, by rights contests, and by reconciling interests. Just as each individual person employs a blend of walk-aways and power plays as his or her own unique individual strategy, each organization is unique too. Every organization employs a blend of power contests, rights contests, and interest reconciliation as its strategy. If it relies more heavily than necessary on power contests, let's call it a *Dominating Organization*. If it relies more heavily than necessary on rights contests, let's call it a *Litigating Organization*. If it relies heavily and appropriately on interest reconciliation, let's call it a *Mediating Organization*.

Is one better than another? Yes indeed! And we'll see why in coming pages. As important, we'll learn what to do about it.

Organizations are populated by employees. Employees are people. People are human. As employees, we bring our

> **Key Term**
>
> **Dominating organization** One in which power contests are the prevailing approach to resolving conflicts.
> **Litigating organization** One in which rights contests are the prevailing approach to resolving conflicts.
> **Mediating organization** One in which interest reconciliation is the prevailing approach to resolving conflicts.

humanity to work with us in the morning and we take it home with us at night. Part of our humanity is our inherited tendency to rely on distancing and coercion (the wrong reflexes) as tactics in our daily rights and power contests. It isn't in our *nature* to place a non-adversarial frame around the fact of divergent interests—our animal ancestors would have died (and so not produced us, their descendants) if they had placed that perceptual frame around the fact of their being a tasty morsel for a nearby predator. Rather, it *is* our nature to frame divergent interests as competing interests—to see differentness as dangerous. Consequently, the "human resources" who constitute a workforce are predisposed to engage in power and rights contests, thereby producing a dominating or litigating organization. It is the enlightened individual who is able to choose the strategy of non-adversarial engagement with others who have differing interests. It is the enlightened organization that can systemically employ interest reconciliation as its strategic approach to resolving workplace conflicts. Enlightened individuals are rare. Mediating Organizations are almost unheard of.

Which Are You?

Use the Dana Diagnostic Survey of Conflict Management Strategies to take a snapshot of your organization. This shortened version of the survey will produce a fuzzy picture, but you might discern a blurry image of the conflict management strategy that is imbedded in your company.

The Dana Diagnostic Survey of Conflict Management Strategies

This survey yields an indication of the prevailing strategy for managing conflict in your organization. A valid diagnosis can be achieved only with proper statistical sampling of employees. However, by responding representatively of others in your organization, a useful illustration may result.

Instructions

1. Write a number from 1 to 7 beside each of the 12 statements below, where 1 = "Not at all true of my organization" and 7 = "Very true of my organization." React to every statement.
2. React as you think things REALLY are, not as you would like them to be.
3. Try to react as you think the typical employee in your organization would. Imagine that everyone in your organization was asked to react to these statements and then write the number you think would be the average of everyone's responses.

Statements

1. Meetings sometimes last longer than planned in order to ensure that everyone agrees with a decision or course of action.
2. Employees complain a lot about things being unfair.
3. The general management style is to increase the pressure on employees when they don't conform to their supervisor's expectations.
4. When one person in a group meeting disagrees with the rest, that person is usually ignored.

5. When employees are in disagreement about a technical issue, they often go to their manager to make the final decision.
6. The feeling that "I don't like it but there's nothing I can do about it" is widespread.
7. When performance appraisals are done, managers generally try to get the employee to agree with the final assessment before ending the discussion.
8. Employees generally respect the right of their managers to make decisions, and willingly go along with them, even if they disagree.
9. It is not uncommon for people to raise their voices when trying to win an argument.
10. Most employees try to resolve disputes with coworkers in a way that everyone accepts.
11. This organization "goes by the book" and relies heavily on "rules and regulations" when handling employee problems.
12. When a dispute arises between coworkers, they often go to other coworkers to try to get others to agree with them.

Scoring
1 For statements 1, 7, and 10, subtract the rating from 8 (this reverses the scale).
2. Add the 12 numbers.
3. Multiple that sum times 1.39.
4. Subtract that result from 116.67.
This calculation yields the *Mediating Strategy Index*.

Next
5. Add the ratings for only statements 2, 5, 8, and 11.
6. Multiply that result by 4.167.
7. Subtract that result from 116.67.
This calculation yields the *Litigating Strategy Index*.

Next
8. Add the ratings for only statements 3, 6, 9, and 12.
9. Multiply that result by 4.167.
10. Subtract that result from 116.67.
This calculation yields the *Dominating Strategy Index*.

Interpretation of Index Scores
Higher index scores mean that the corresponding conflict management strategy is more likely to be imbedded in the organization's culture, structure, and employee competencies.

Converting Index Scores to Quintiles
81-100 = Fifth quintile = Predominant use of this strategy
61-80 = Fourth quintile = Significant use
41-60 = Third quintile = Moderate use
21-40 = Second quintile = Infrequent use
1-20 = First quintile = Rare use

Your scores should be regarded only as illustrative. No strategic executive decisions should be made on this information alone. To the degree that your scores are indicative of the actual conflict management strategy that is imbedded within your organization, the following general conclusions may be drawn:

1. Higher quintile ranking of the Mediating Strategy indicates greater organizational effectiveness.
2. Higher quintile rankings of the Litigating and Dominating Strategies indicate lower organizational effectiveness.
3. Rankings in the third quintile or below on Mediating Strategy suggest that substantial costs and risks, and sub-optimal decision quality, are present in the organization. This conclusion is strengthened if the rankings on Litigating and/or Dominating Strategies are in the fourth quintile or higher.
4. Rankings in the fourth quintile or above on Mediating Strategy suggest a favorable state of organizational health and effectiveness. This conclusion is strengthened if the rankings on Litigating and/or Dominating Strategies are in the second quintile or lower.

Seamus distributed the survey to a hundred employees who represent a microcosm of MTI. He included employees in all occupational groups, all cultural, linguistic, and ethnic categories, and all service sectors of the company. With this cross-section, he was able to estimate how the whole company might respond if all 20 thousand employees answered the questions. The resulting mean index scores of his sample are: Dominating Index = 19, Litigating Index = 55, Mediating Index = 74.

He's pleased that MTI's employees rely so little on power contests to resolve workplace disputes. And he's pleased that the mediating index is much higher than in most organizations. But he's concerned that employees rely heavily on rights contests. In particular, the mean ratings of questions 8 and 11 are high, suggesting that employees have difficulty disagreeing with their managers and that the company has become rule-bound. "Maybe it's inevitable that, with our explosive growth, people feel like they have to go by the book since there's little accumulated experience to guide them," Seamus muses. "But still, I wonder if there's a connection between the scary results of the conflict cost instrument and the high litigating index?"

Seamus is thinking like a scientist. He recognizes the possible causal link between the prevalence of power contests and the financial cost of conflict in his company. He also recognizes that unmanaged conflict is a causal factor in the risks of really, really bad things happening—the "torpedo submarines in our midst" that we discussed toward the end of Chapter 2. But he's not too worried about torpedoes blowing up the S.S. MTI. He's confident that its crew is mindful of the early warning signals. (Can you be as confident about your organization?)

Decision-Making

But Seamus is a bit concerned that subtle conflict might be affecting how decisions are made throughout MTI. After all, being in a flat organization, most employees work in self-directed teams. And, they have high decision-making authority, although they lean heavily on others for information in making those decisions. They're very interdependent. He considers two ways that conflict can erode good decision-making:

1. Every solo decision-maker needs information from others to make the best decision. When information providers are in conflict with the decision-maker, the information they provide is inevitably distorted.
2. When two or more people share responsibility for making a decision, conflict between them makes their decision susceptible to being influenced by their rights or power contest. Their objectivity in jointly deciding what is best for the company is compromised.

Seamus recalls a recent interaction between Gabriela, the Director of Environmental Mediation Training for Latin America, and Bart, Vice President for Government Services Global. Last week, Seamus arranged a video Internet conference call to improve coordination between MTI's environmental mediation training services and government officials worldwide. Gabriela's counterparts in other regions around the world also participated. During the discussion, she asked Bart for his advice about how to approach the Costa Rican Minister of the Environment. Seamus sensed that Bart wasn't as forthcoming as he could have been, but didn't think much of it at the time. In retrospect, he muses, "I wonder if there is some tension between Bart and Gabriela that resulted in his not giving her his best advice? Might he have been withholding information as a walk-away? Might there be a subtle retaliatory cycle going on between them? Might they be failing to use preventive mediation to break the cycle? If so, the success of our environmental training programs in Costa Rica might be jeopardized."

Seamus is beginning to think about nudging MTI toward being more of a Mediating Organization and less of a Litigating Organization. "We might be paying a price that I didn't know we are paying," he reflects. "But our twenty thousand employees are already skilled in mediation. Our staff have plenty of conflict resolution competencies. What else is needed?"

The Three Dimensions

Seamus may be entirely correct about MTI's workforce having all the competencies they need to skillfully manage conflict at every level, off-line and on-line. (Few organizations could say the same.) Developing mediation competencies has been the focus of this book up to now. We've mastered the four mediation tools. But competencies are only one-third of the puzzle. The remaining two-thirds are "structure" and "culture."

Each person's individual conflict management strategy—that idiosyncratic blend of our favorite and long-practiced walk-aways and power plays—is imbedded in dimensions of ourselves that we have little awareness of. Likewise, an organization's conflict management strategy is imbedded in dimensions of itself in ways that even its top executives are seldom aware of.

Providing competencies by means of training is seldom sufficient to transform an organization. The world's largest professional association of corporate trainers, the American Society for Training and Development, realized this disturbing truth years ago and has responded by broadening its focus beyond training alone. Trainers often make stellar presentations about important workplace skills and ... plop! Nothing happens. Participants' evaluations are great, but there's no on-the-job impact. Trainees enjoy the classroom experience, but when they go back to work, it's as if they never left. Why?

> **Key Term**
>
> **Three dimensions** The areas in every organization in which its conflict management strategy is imbedded.
> **Competencies** Employees' abilities to manage conflict.
> **Structure** Formal design of the organizational system.
> **Culture** Norms, shared values, and attitudes that influence workplace conflict behavior.

Structure

Every organization of any size has a structure. That is, its founders, designers, and leaders have designed systems, procedures, policies, and formalized practices that are intended to get the work done effectively and efficiently. In fact, structure is what makes organizations organized. The organization chart that reflects its reporting hierarchy is part of structure. Job descriptions are part of structure. The compensation system is part of structure. The performance appraisal system is part of structure. We could list hundreds of other elements of any organization that have resulted from someone at some time saying, "We need to have a way to ...," and then designing a way to do it.

Organizations need structure. Otherwise, total anarchy would reign. It would be complete chaos. We need order. But might parts of that structure get in the way of resolving conflicts by means of reconciling interests?

Seamus thinks about the structure of MTI. As such a large organization, it absolutely must be structured. People need definition of the tasks they are hired to perform—hence job descriptions. People need leadership—hence hierarchy. People need clarity about how much and when they are paid, as well as extrinsic incentives to do their jobs—hence a compensation system. People need feedback about how well they are doing, and guidance about how to do better—hence performance reviews.

"But I wonder if some aspects of MTI's structure prevent us from using the conflict resolution competencies that our employees have?" Seamus reflects.

Seamus remembers Kyle, the grouchy ward clerk at Patients-R-Us Hospital, whose rebuff to coworkers' requests was "That's not my job, so it must be yours." "Seems to me that Kyle's job description, or at least his understanding of it, was too narrow," thinks Seamus. "If his job description had included 'Use self-help mediation tools to prevent and resolve conflicts with coworkers,' Kyle clearly wasn't doing his job. Did Nan or his previous supervisors review his performance against this job expectation? Was his compensation affected by the results of his performance of that job expectation? If not, that element of the hospital's structure was an obstacle to the use of conflict management competencies, even if Kyle had received training in how to use workplace mediation tools."

Roadblocks

Smart Managing   Ask yourself, "What blocks me from using the four self-help mediation tools in my job?" Ask your employees the same question. Your answer, and theirs, will point you toward structural and cultural obstacles to using conflict resolution competencies.

Seamus presses the scanback key on his e-book to review other conflicts that were discussed in earlier chapters. Many of them contain clues that, even if employees possessed the competencies, the organization's structure posed barriers to their use. "How can I identify and remove the structural obstacles to effective conflict management in MTI?" he asks himself. No easy answer comes to mind yet. Gotta keep reading, Seamus.

Culture

Just as every organization of any size has structure, it also has culture. Its members share certain values, attitudes, and behavioral norms. Organizational culture is extremely complex, and most of its prescriptions and proscriptions are not within the awareness of its members. That is, we aren't aware of what the culture is telling us to do and not to do. Unless we deviate greatly from these cultural expectations, we act as we do because it just seems right, normal, and appropriate. We don't think much about acting or thinking differently.

Puzzle: What was the last animal to discover water? Answer: Fish. When we are so immersed in an environment and feel so at home within it, we don't know it's there. Those of us who get along comfortably in our society do so because we conform to the behavioral and attitudinal expectations of our societal culture. We share deep values with others and seldom question them because we rarely encounter people who don't share them with us. When we meet individuals who deviate from those norms, we dismiss them as defective individuals. We mutter to ourselves, "How could anyone not believe in democracy? How could anyone think terrorism is OK? How could anyone not know that monogamy is right and polygamy is wrong? How could anyone not believe in God?"

Our answer? "They must be crazy. They must be stupid. They must be primitive heathens who haven't been educated." But there are entire societies of people who share the polar opposite of these "obvious" truths. Did all the crazy, stupid people just happen to be born into those societies? No. People with the same native intelligence and capabilities as you and I can conform to the norms of a culture that is shockingly different from our own— just as we conform to ours. And—here's the shocker—you and I would have conformed to their culture if we'd been born into it. That would have been the water we swim in.

Organizational cultures operate in precisely the same way as societal cultures. Organizations convey to their members, by both explicit and implicit messages, what is expected of us. How should we act? How should we think? What should be believe? The teeth in these messages that enforce our compliance is "If you don't conform, you won't fit in, you won't be liked, and you won't succeed." We get the message. We conform. Or, if we are unable to conform, we move on in search of a workplace culture that feels like home. And our conformance is almost entirely unconscious. We are a fish in water, blissfully ignorant that it's there.

Seamus wonders, "Are there widely or universally held norms, values, attitudes, and social expectations within MTI that block the use of employees' conflict management competencies?"

He scans back in his e-book to review Shawna's mediation of a team conflict in the General Case Study Company in Chapter 6. Her team members were acutely worried that they might be blamed for causing GCSC's failure to meet its customer's quality criteria. Their worry led to finger-pointing at others on the team for being at fault. "Hmmm...," Seamus muses, "It seems to me there was a norm within GCSC that mistakes were unacceptable and that making them would draw

Know Yourself, Know Your Culture

Smart Managing   Ask yourself, "How do I need to conduct myself to be accepted and approved of around here? What attitudes and values can I freely express, confident that I won't be criticized? What attitudes and values do I keep to myself for fear that others would disapprove?" Your answers provide a glimpse of your organization's culture. (Resist the temptation to reply, "I don't conform. My beliefs are my own. It's what I truly think. I'm my own person. I determine my own opinions, attitudes, and values." Those replies simply reveal that *you don't know that you don't know* that you are largely a product of your culture.) Next, ask yourself, "Specifically, what conflict-related behaviors, attitudes, and values can I express and must I not express in order to fit in?" Your answers point to cultural obstacles to using conflict resolution competencies.

unforgiving criticism. But, looking back over my long career, I've learned a lot from the mistakes I've made—they've been valuable sources of learning. I wonder if GCSC's culture prevented employees from learning by their mistakes because of the way they handled conflict?"

Seamus the scientist is now examining the possible causal link between a specific cultural norm in GCSC and the company's effectiveness. His attention shifts from GCSC to MTI. "How can I identify and remove the cultural obstacles to effective conflict management in MTI," he asks himself. Still, no easy answer comes to mind. Gotta keep reading, Seamus.

Getting from Here to There

Seamus is at a loss to find expert guidance in applying this new concept of strategic management of organizational conflict to his own company. Then it occurs to him that, if anyone in the world knows how to do this, then someone in MTI should know something about it. So, he sends an email to all subject matter experts in the company, asking if anyone is knowledgeable about this cutting-edge conflict management technology.

"I am," replies Susan within minutes of Seamus' query popping up on her computer screen. (Yes, this is the same Susan we briefly visited early in Chapter 1 who was involved in

---

The Six Steps of Becoming a Mediating Organization   TOOLS

Step 1. Assessment—Diagnose the currently embedded conflict management strategy.

Step 2. Planning—Form, authorize, and train an advisory group.

Step 3. Establish core competencies—Learn workplace mediation tools.

Step 4. Modify structure—Locate and remove obstacles to interest-based conflict management.

Step 5. Modify culture—Replace counter-constructive norms with positive ones.

Step 6. Reassessment—Measure progress toward a Mediating Organization.

a technical disagreement with her colleague, Sean.) She joined MTI several years ago as a trainer of managerial mediation in the Corporate Division, and is now based in Boston. Susan's e-mial continues, "I've done some research on the topic, and am keenly interested in its potential as a new service in the Corporate Division. In fact, I've met with the author of the book you're reading. At the risk of seeming immodest, I believe I know as much about strategic conflict management as Dr. Dana does."

Seamus immediately places a voice call to Susan. After several minutes he's impressed with her comprehension of the subject. "Great!" he exclaims to himself. "I've got an expert right here in my own company. Let's get to work on this." He arranges for Susan to come to Washington to get started.

Step 1. Assessment: *Diagnose the current conflict management strategy.*
Susan's first recommendation is to get a more complete understanding of the strategy that is currently imbedded in the three dimensions of MTI—its employee competencies, its structure, and its culture. She suggests administering the complete version of the Dana Diagnostic Survey to a larger sample of its employees than the hundred who provided Seamus' initial snapshot.

"We can get a good picture of the strategy in the whole company from as few as 5% of the total employee population as long as we're careful with our sampling," Susan explains. "We must ensure that every employee is represented in the sample. And, we want to be sure that there are enough responses from each division, each hierarchical level, each ethnic and linguistic category, each country, and each occupational group to let us do statistical comparisons among them," she continues. "We'll probably find significant differences in conflict strategies in the different parts of the MTI organization. Knowing what those differences are will enable us to identify and remove structural and cultural obstacles that may exist in one part of the company and not in another."

Finally, Susan makes an important point to Seamus, the CEO of the company that employs her. "This project is similar in many ways to organization development, or 'OD,' projects, which are often carried out by external consultants. One advantage of being external to the client company is that the consultant can be independent of political pressures that might affect an internal employee, even if that employee were fully competent to provide the consultation. Another is that members of the client organization are more likely to view the external consultant as objective and unbiased, and will therefore trust the process and take it seriously. I would like to have your assurance that I have your full support to undertake this project as independently as if I were not employed by MTI. Does that make sense to you?" Seamus perfectly understands Susan's concerns and gives her his assurance. He authorizes her to proceed.

In just a couple of weeks, Susan has selected a representative sample of one thousand (5%) of MTI's employees who constitute a microcosm of the company. She has sent the diagnostic survey electronically to the selected employees, accompanied by a note from Seamus explaining the purpose of the effort and asking for their cooperation. She also has prepared a note for MTI's monthly e-newsletter, which all 20,000 employees receive, inviting them to visit the company's Web site for a full explanation of the project. She promises to post regular progress reports on the Web so all employees can monitor any activities that might affect them.

Only a week later, the completed surveys have been returned from respondents around the world. Susan crunches the numbers and prepares a report with detailed stats. A high-resolution photo of MTI's conflict management strategy has now been taken and it's ready for viewing.

Step 2. Planning: *Form, authorize, and train an advisory group.*
Even while assessment was under way, Susan began forming an advisory group (let's call it the "AG") that would act as a steering committee to help her analyze data, make decisions, and prepare action plans throughout the project. Like the sample of the workforce that was selected to respond to the survey,

the advisory group was a microcosm of MTI. But instead of a thousand individuals, the AG has about a dozen. Nevertheless, Susan's intent is to form a group that can represent the interests and concerns of the entire workforce. She asked Seamus to be a member of the AG, but he would have no more authority than any other member.

Communication channels are set up so individuals within the constituency represented by each member of the AG can bring their ideas to his or her attention. For example, Vladimir, who is a program administrator based in Novosibirsk, is the AG's contact point for the 2500 program administrators worldwide as well as for all staff in countries of the former Soviet Union and for all Russian-speaking employees worldwide. Similarly, Chidinma, a conflict coach based in Lagos, Nigeria, is the AG's contact for all coaches worldwide and for all staff located in sub-Saharan Africa.

A same-time/same-place launch meeting was held in Dubai, a convenient travel destination for AG members located in Europe, Africa, and Asia. At that meeting Seamus confirmed the AG's authority to guide the project under Susan's direction. Had MTI been a company in any other industry, Susan would have conducted training in workplace mediation tools so the AG would have full knowledge of the competencies that would be developed throughout the company. But since MTI's employees already possess these competencies, only a brief overview was needed. Finally, Susan facilitated a planning process similar to an ordinary strategic planning retreat. Following the Dubai meeting, communication among members of the AG would be done electronically—same-time/different-place or different-time/different-place.

Susan is now ready to implement the plan.

Step 3. Establish Core Competencies: *Learn workplace mediation tools.*
The AG decided to begin with a pilot project in one region, rather than attempt to roll out the program worldwide. Europe was selected as the pilot, due to its compact geography and its diversity of languages and cultures. For these reasons, AG felt

that the European Region would be most representative of the entire company. Susan and the AG expected that by debugging the European pilot they could prevent many bugs from appearing later, when the program was extended to other regions.

Because of its employees' existing expertise in workplace mediation, little additional training in the core competencies was required. If MTI had been a manufacturing firm or a bank or a government agency, broadbased training in those competencies would have been necessary. Happily for Seamus, only some refresher programs for administrative and support staff were needed. Susan and the AG decided to enlist the services of one trainer in each language in Europe to provide the refreshers. They accomplished this in under three months. An on-line achievement test was administered, which confirmed that all staff had sufficiently acquired the competencies.

Susan is now ready to identify obstacles to the use of those competencies.

Step 4, Modify Structure: *Locate and remove obstacles to interest-based conflict management.*

Step 5: Modify Culture: *Replace counter-constructive norms with positive ones.*
Steps 4 and 5 are carried out concurrently. Members of the AG asked their constituents in Europe to nominate colleagues who possess excellent interviewing skills. Susan met with the nominees in Brussels and selected 10 interviewers, ensuring that each European language was spoken fluently by at least one interviewer. Susan then trained the interviewers to gather information from a representative sample of all 3,000 employees in Europe. Specifically, she trained them to listen to answers to a series of questions, and to follow up those answers with more probing questions. A sample of the questions that interviewers were trained to ask is:

Have you used self-mediation in the past month?
If so,
• What was the situation, briefly?

- What difficulties did you encounter?
- How successful do you think it was?
- What prevented it from being more successful?
- If you could change one aspect of your work setting that might have made the mediation more successful, what would it be?

(Ask other probing follow-up questions to uncover obstacles that prevented successful use of self-mediation.)

If not,

- Why not?
- If it seemed to you that there has been no conflict signif-icant enough to use self-mediation, how confident are you that your judgment about its low significance is not a walk-away? (Probe the answer sensitively and non-judgmentally.)
- If there has been a conflict that might have been resolved off-line and you did not use self-mediation, what prevent-ed you from doing so?
- If you could change one aspect of your work setting that might have made it easier for you to use mediation, what would it be? Don't be concerned about how practical and feasible your idea might be. Just think of things that could have made it easier.

(Ask other probing follow-up questions to uncover obstacles that prevented the use of self-mediation.)

Other more targeted questions were created drawing on findings of specific issues uncovered by analysis of results of the assessment survey administered in Step 1.

Once interviewer training was completed, an interview schedule was developed and the interviewers were deployed throughout Europe. Interviewers filed daily reports by email. Susan's support staff converted the data into a statistical pro-gram. Although interview data were mostly qualitative, the stats program was able to quantify some dimensions, such as the fre-quency that a specific obstacle was mentioned. For example, "lack of time" was mentioned by 34% of interview subjects when asked the question "If not, why not?"

In a few weeks all interviews were completed and data had been analyzed. The summary report revealed a large number of perceived obstacles to using workplace mediation tools, which were listed in order of frequency. Susan's first task is to separate the structural obstacles from the cultural obstacles. Here is the beginning of her list under the two categories of obstacles:

Structural Obstacles

- *Low accountability.* MTI's performance review procedure does not include discussion of missed opportunities to do mediation.
- *Limited same-time/same-place opportunity.* Most employees work from home, so there are few convenient occasions to have face-to-face dialogue.
- *Little time.* Due to the burgeoning demand for mediation training services, most employees are stretched to the limit to get work done in the time available.

Cultural Obstacles

- *Low openness for volunteering feedback.* Employees often observe situations where colleagues should use mediation, but, because they are not personally involved, do not feel free to share their observations with those who are involved.
- *Denial.* Because MTI's employees regard themselves as expert conflict resolvers, it is difficult to admit when conflicts emerge and need to be addressed off-line. They worry that such admissions would appear to be admissions of incompetence.
- *Competitiveness.* Trainers who achieve high participant evaluations often openly brag about them. A status hierarchy based on trainer evals has evolved. Consequently, employees who receive acceptable but lower evaluations feel unfree to initiate self-mediation with high performers, even on unrelated issues.

Susan distributes the report of interview results to the AG

and asks them to gather ideas from their constituencies that may contribute to solutions. Susan suggests that they consider only the top three most critical and prevalent obstacles of each type—structural and cultural. Lower-ranking obstacles will be addressed later.

Taking advantage of MTI's virtual meeting technology, Susan convenes a same-time/different-place meeting of the AG to use force field analysis (originated by social psychologist Kurt Lewin in the 1940s) to develop an action plan. In olden days, this had to be done same-time/same-place with endless sheets of flipchart paper taped to the walls of conference rooms.

As you see, redesigning the conflict management strategy of a large organization is a tedious enterprise. Since this is a brief-case book, and not an encyclopedia, we'll illustrate just one shortened force field analysis of just one of the obstacles that Susan's AG identified.

Cultural Obstacle: Low openness for volunteering feedback.
Driving Forces
- Employees are skilled at recognizing conflict when they see it.
- Employees who might give unsolicited feedback are skilled in being assertive, not aggressive, in expressing their concerns to others.

Key Term

Force field analysis A problem-solving and action-planning technique that involves identifying "driving forces" and "restraining forces" that are affecting why something is the way it is at the present time—the status quo.

The forces of each type are then identified and prioritized according to their impact on the status quo and their susceptibility to change. The problem-solvers then brainstorm possible ways to strengthen driving forces (toward the desired goal) and ways to weaken restraining forces (away from the desired goal). These ideas are then tested for practicality and usefulness. Those that are found to be practical and useful are incorporated into an action plan that defines who will do what by when.

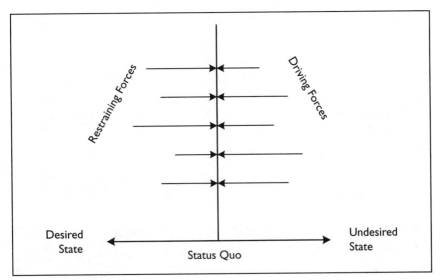

Figure 8-1. Force field analysis

- Employees who might receive unsolicited feedback are skilled in the "owning my own experience" thinking tool (ref Chapter 7).

Restraining Forces
- People who are drawn to the field of mediation are typically "nice" people who don't want to offend the feelings of others.
- It's easier and safer for employees to "pretend I didn't see" evidence of acting out behavior by a colleague.
- There's no accountability that makes coworkers responsible for giving unsolicited feedback when they observe behavior that suggests a retaliatory cycle is under way.

Once the forces that produce the status quo are identified and prioritized, Susan and the AG proceed to build an action plan.

Action Plan
Strengthen driving forces: Maintain existing skills through periodic in-service workshops and on-line reviews.

Weaken restraining forces: CEO Seamus will send a message

to all employees via the monthly e-newsletter that:

- acknowledges the norm in MTI's corporate culture that makes employees less open about giving unsolicited feedback when they observe conflicts between others,
- explains the financial price that MTI pays for this norm,
- expresses appreciation for the humanistic values of MTI's staff, exemplified by the desire to not offend others' feelings,
- asks team leaders and other supervisory staff to raise discussion of this issue in their regular staff meetings, and
- announces that the performance review process will be modified to include discussion of giving unsolicited feedback.

Susan's pilot project in the European region produces a 50-page action plan that specifies who is responsible for performing each task, gives time markers and deadlines for its completion, and identifies specific supporting resources that others will provide. No less importantly, it includes a clear plan for implementation so there is no ambiguity about what will be done. (Notice the resemblance of the action plan to the deal that culminates the off-line mediation tools described in earlier chapters.)

Step 6. Reassessment: *Measure progress toward a Mediating Organization.*

The European region pilot has been implemented. The AG's action plan calls for re-administration of the Dana Diagnostic Survey of Conflict Management Strategies six months after implementation is begun. Results show movement toward a Mediating Organization in Europe, while there has been no change elsewhere. This proves to Seamus that the pilot has been a success, so he asks Susan extend it to roll it out to other regions.

Strategic Management of Conflict on a Smaller Scale

Most readers do not have the scope of responsibilities that Seamus does as CEO of an $8 billion company with 20,000 employees in 24 time zones. What if you run a much smaller operation? What if you are the leader of a team of 10?

Even your small team has competencies, structure, and culture. As a team leader, you may have less control over budget for imparting competencies than Seamus did. You may have less authority for modifying structure than Seamus did. And, the culture of your team, being a part of the surrounding corporate culture, may be less independent from its environment than MTI's culture.

But the same principles that Susan demonstrated for us at MTI apply to you. Fortunately, your undertaking to change the conflict management strategy in your smaller corner of the world will be dramatically easier and quicker.

Making a Difference

Everyone wants to make a difference. As parents, we want to help our children grow into successful, happy adults. As managers, we want to help our employees grow in their careers while they fulfill their responsibilities under our leadership. As organization members, we want to contribute to the success of the enterprise. Ultimately, we want to leave the world a better place than we found it.

Your humble author also wants to make a difference. The tools found in this book are now in your toolbox. They are practical, proven tools. Have confidence in their utility. Have the courage to use them. I've done my best to deliver them to your toolbox. Now it's up to you. What will it be? The hammer? Or this new gadget?

Manager's Checklist for Chapter 8

❑ Conflict management is a strategic business issue.

❏ Employee competencies alone do not ensure an effective organization. Structural and cultural obstacles that block their use must be identified and removed.

❏ Every organization has a conflict management strategy composed of a blend of contesting power, contesting rights, and reconciling interests.

❏ Costs, risks, and decision quality are negatively affected by a conflict management strategy that too heavily relies on power and rights contests, and under-utilizes reconciliation of interests.

❏ A six-step procedure can be used to move your organization, large or small, from a dominating strategy (power-based) and a litigating strategy (rights-based) toward a mediating strategy (interest-based).

Conflict
Resolution

Index